STECK-VA

PAIR-IT BOOKS®

FICTION AND NONFICTION FOR PROFICIENT READERS

TEACHER'S GUIDE

Proficiency Stage 5

Reviewers

Dr. Gail Choice
Assistant Principal
Sanford, Florida

Roz German
Director of Literacy (IA), Community School District 23
Brooklyn, New York

Becky Koesel
Third Grade Teacher
Gladewater, Texas

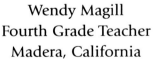

Wendy Magill
Fourth Grade Teacher
Madera, California

STECK-VAUGHN
ELEMENTARY · SECONDARY · ADULT · LIBRARY
® A Harcourt Classroom Education Company

www.steck-vaughn.com

ACKNOWLEDGMENTS

Executive Editor	Stephanie Muller
Senior Editors	Kristy Schulz, Amanda Sperry
Supervising Designer	Pamela Heaney
Designers	Cindi Ellis, Christine Grether
Electronic Production Artist	Donna Brawley
Electronic Production	Rmedia
Editorial Development	The Quarasan Group, Inc.

Photography: (abbreviations: BC: Bruce Coleman, Inc.; CB: Corbis; GH: Grant Heilman Photography; PA: Peter Arnold, Inc.; PD: PhotoDisc; TSM: The Stock Market; TSI: Tony Stone Images)

Front Cover (beaver) ©Stanley Schoenberger/GH, (experiment) Rick Williams, (shoes) ©A. Berg/Spooner/Gamma Liaison, (dragonfly) ©John Cancalosi/PA, (deer) ©Erwin & Peggy Bauer/BC; Back Cover (doe) CB/Tom Brakefield, (anemone) ©Stuart Westmorland/TSI, (boots) CB/Bettmann, (basilisk) CB/Joe McDonald; p.1 (l) CB/Joe McDonald; p.1 (tr) ©Douglas Faulkner/TSM; pp.1 (br) 2 (t) Rick Williams; p.2 (b) ©PD; p.3 (l) CB/Kevin Schafer; p.3 (m) Archive Photos; p.3 (r) ©Arthur C. Smith/GH; p.4 (l) ©Stuart Westmorland/TSI; pp.4 (r), 5 (l), 5 (r), 6 (br), 7 (tr), 7 (m) Park Street; p.6 (tr) Digital Studios; p.6 (m) CORBIS/Ian Cartwright, Frank Lane Picture Agency; p.7 (bl) ©A. Berg/Spooner/Gamma Liaison; p.7 (br) Courtesy Bata Shoe Museum; p.10 (t) ©PD; p.10 (b) Park Street; p.11 (t) ©Darrell Gullen/TSI; p.11 (b) ©Norbert Wu/PA; p.12 (l) Park Street; p.12 (r) ©Stuart Westmorland/TSI; p.13 (t) CB/Stephen Frink; p.13 (bl) ©John Cancalosi/PA; pp.13 (br), 14 (b) Park Street; p.14 (t) ©Darrell Gullen/TSI; pp.15 (t), 18 (forest) ©W. Geiersperger/TSM, (buck) ©Erwin & Peggy Bauer/BC, (fox, doe) CB/Tom Brakefield, (beaver) ©Stanley Schoenberger/GH, (owl) ©Art Wolfe/TSI, (chipmunk) ©Arthur C. Smith/GH; p.15 (b) ©Arthur C. Smith/GH; p.17 CB/Tom Brakefield; pp.21 (t), 24 (children) ©Mug Shots/TSM, (tools) ©PD; p.21 (b) ©PD; p.23 ©Mug Shots/TSM; pp.27 (t), 30 Cover (basilisk) CB/Joe McDonald, (tarsier) CB/Kevin Schafer, (leaf insect) Frank Lane Picture Agency, (hoatzin) CB/Kevin Schafer; ; p.27 (b) ©Zefa Germany/TSM; p.29 CB/Kevin Schafer; pp.33, 36 Cover: (Ringgold) AP/Wide World Photos, (Picasso) Roger-Violet/The Bridgeman Art Library, (O'Keefe) AP/Wide World Photos, (Peña) Photo by Jim Arndt, Courtesy Amado M. Peña, Jr., (Ney) Elisabet Ney in Smock, circa 1859, Courtesy of Elisabet Ney Museum, Austin, Texas, (Woodruff) SC-CN-86-0050 Schomburg Center for Research in Black Culture; p.33 "Mestizo Series: Los Aresanos" Artwork Courtesy of Amado M. Pena Jr.; p.35 Roger-Violet/The Bridgeman Art Library; pp.39 (t), 42 ©John Cancalosi/PA; p.45 (t) ©PD; p.45 (b) ©Robert Pearcy/Animals Animals; p.47 ©Barbara Reed/Animals Animals; p.48 ©PD; pp.51 (t), 54 (moccasins) ©Christie's Images, (gold boots) Courtesy Bata Shoe Museum, (pattens) Courtesy Bata Shoe Museum, (tennis shoes) ©Stockbyte, (doc martens) ©A. Berg/Spooner/Gamma Liaison; p.51 (b) CB/Bettmann; p.53 Musee du Louvre, Paris/Explorer, Paris/SuperStock; p.57 (t) ©PD; p.57 (b) ©Tom Brakefield/BRAKE/BC; p.59 ©Roland Seitre/PA; p.60 ©PD; p.63 (t), ©Darrell Gulin/TSI; p.63 (b) ©Norbert Wu/PA; p.65 CB/Stephen Frink; p.66 (t) ©Darrell Gulin/TSI; p.69 (t) CB/Minnesota Historical Society; pp.69 (b), 71 ©The Bridgeman Art Library; p.72 (t) CB/Minnesota Historical Society; pp.75, 78 (globe) ©PD, (Easter Island) ©Tom Till/TSI, (France) CB/Craig Aurness, (Greece) CB/Kevin Schafer, (Guatemala) ©Jose Fuste Raga/TSM, (Italy, India) ©Superstock; pp.75 (b), 77 ©Tom Till/TSI; p.81 (t) ©Richard A. Cooke II/TSI; p.81 (b) CB/Earl Kowall; p.83 ©Scott Melcer; p.84 ©Richard A. Cooke II/TSI; p.87 ©Charles Bupton/Stock Boston; p.89 (b) ©Tony Freeman/PhotoEdit; p.93 ©PD; p.93 (b) ©PD; p.95 ©John Sanford/Science Photo Library/Photo Researchers; p.96 ©PD; p.99 NASA; p.101 Courtesy Ethel Bolden; p.102 NASA.

Illustrations: Cindy Aarvig

Pair-it Books® is a registered trademark of Steck-Vaughn Company.

Steck-Vaughn Company grants you permission to duplicate enough copies of blackline masters to distribute to your students.

ISBN 0-7398-0919-9

Copyright © 2000 Steck-Vaughn Company

All rights reserved. No part of the material protected by this copyright may be reproduced or utilized in any form or by any means, electronic or mechanical, including photocopying, recording, or by any information storage and retrieval system, without permission in writing from the copyright owner. Requests for permission to make copies of any part of the work should be mailed to: Copyrights Permissions, Steck-Vaughn Company, P.O. Box 26015, Austin, Texas 78755.

Printed in the United States of America.

2 3 4 5 6 7 8 9 B 03 02 01

CONTENTS

Proficiency Stage 5: Lessons and Take It Home Letters

PROGRAM OVERVIEW

Reading can open doors of interest, mystery, and excitement for students. Have you ever noticed that after a student reads a fiction story about a sport or animal, he or she suddenly wants to know more about other sports or animals? Then that student needs an informational book to read—a nonfiction book that is on the same reading level and is as interesting as the fiction book. This pairing is the premise behind the *Steck-Vaughn Pair-It Books®* series.

Pair-It Books® is an emergent through proficiency reading program of companion fiction and nonfiction books paired by topic and reading level. *Pair-It Books* help students move from reading fictional narratives to reading nonfiction for information. This series of books eases students with that transition. In addition, the reading of nonfiction text helps prepare students for some standardized tests.

Using paired books will motivate young readers. Students can practice and apply specific strategies as they read both kinds of books on a topic. Each pair has a strong matching of text and visuals to support the comprehension process. The common content of both books allows readers to use prior knowledge to build on what they know. Reading informational texts becomes an extension of reading fictional narratives.

Because students read at different levels, there are six stages of *Pair-It Books* that build upon one another. The Early Emergent stage consists of eight-page books. These books lay the groundwork for beginning readers with rhythm, rhyme, repetition, and alliteration. The Emergent Stage 1 consists of eight-page books as well. These books are predictable and repetitive in nature, with a strong matching of art or photos to support the text. Emergent Stage 2 books, each with sixteen pages, gradually become more difficult and reflect more complex text structures, including dialogue, content vocabulary, and question-and-answer format.

Early Fluency Stage 3 provides sixteen-page and twenty-four page books that introduce readers to these genres: fables, folktales, tall tales, poems, and pourquoi tales. In the twenty-four page books, the matching of pictures and text is supported by the use of chapters, indexes, and glossaries. Fluency Stage 4 includes twenty-four and thirty-two page books that allow readers to experience lengthier text. In these books, readers encounter different genres. These books also include photos with captions, chapters, glossaries, and indexes.

Proficiency Stage 5 consists of thirty-two and forty page books. The fictional chapter books cover genres such as fantasy, pourquoi tales, journals, mysteries, and diaries. These fiction books give developing readers opportunities to relate to characters, plots, and settings. The nonfiction books are also chapter books, with captions for photos, timelines, tables, glossaries, charts, maps, diagrams, and indexes. These books give developing readers opportunities to read for new information or to explore interesting topics for individual pleasure reading.

CLASSROOM MANAGEMENT

There are three ways to manage *Pair-It Books* in the classroom.

1. Whole Class Instruction. You may demonstrate specific reading strategies or share books with the whole class.
2. Group Instruction. You may use specific program components with a group of students to teach a reading strategy, a language skill, or a phonics or word study skill.
3. Paired or Independent Instruction. Students explore selected books from the program in pairs or independently.

TYPES OF READING

SHARED READING

Shared reading helps students hear language and how it works in different kinds of texts. When part of a book is read aloud, students can focus on listening to the author's words. Students can listen for language patterns, story structure, sounds of words, and new vocabulary. Students can also review the art or photos that support the text. This will help students with overall comprehension. Finally, after part of a book has been shared, students may feel comfortable with the story and be ready to read the entire book independently.

GUIDED READING

Guided reading helps students use strategies to become more independent readers. It allows students to use reading strategies that enable them to decode and recognize language patterns, new vocabulary, genres, and to become familiar with reading more complex text.

Guided reading begins with an introduction to the book and its components. This may be done through a questioning format to access students' prior knowledge about the topic. Before and during the reading of the book, involve students in making predictions about what they will learn. This gives young readers an insight into developing independent strategies of making and confirming predictions and word study skills.

The next step is individual reading of the book.

During this reading, make sure students are on task, supporting individuals when necessary. During guided reading many teachers often post questions for young readers to think about as they read. These questions allow for points of discussion after reading the book.

The guided reading lesson may include a follow-up activity. Follow-up activities can include writing, art, or discussions that pertain to the text of the book. Guided reading helps young readers take ownership of the strategies to apply to other books, so that reading becomes independent. This fosters independent reading for pleasure and for specific information.

DIRECTED READING

Directed reading helps students build skills and strategies. Mini lessons presenting a specific reading strategy can be used with a small group of students or a large group. The mini lessons area is used to build skills in the areas of reading comprehension, genre recognition, literary components, study skills, phonics, and word study. Once students are familiar with the book and its topic, directed reading can be done at any time.

INDEPENDENT READING

Independent reading occurs when students are capable of reading a book on their own, making their own selections, and reading the book for comprehension. Independent reading allows the young reader to practice reading strategies and to read for pleasure. This kind of reading gives students confidence and promotes self-esteem.

PROGRAM COMPONENTS

THIRTY STUDENT PAIR-IT BOOKS

There are thirty student books, representing fifteen topic-based pairs, in the Proficiency Stage. In each pair, one title is fiction, and one is non-fiction. Several pairs may be combined to present a particular theme to students. For example, an animals thematic unit could include the pairs on amazing animals, dogs, and wild cats.

The Stage 5 books provide opportunities for students to read independently, in small groups, or as a whole class. The books are written in such a way that they can be used as models for students to write their own stories and informational texts.

The books in this stage have some important text-structured features, such as diagrams, time lines, charts, tables, captions, journal entries, and maps. Information learned from the text can be reviewed and extended with the text-structured features. This helps students become familiar with different ways that text can be presented. These features can be used to point out examples from skill lessons and to check comprehension.

TEACHER'S GUIDE

This 112-page Teacher's Guide provides suggestions for introducing the pairs of books as well as lessons that develop phonics skills, word study skills, comprehension strategies, genre recognition, literary components, study skills, and language skills. The Teacher's Guide also includes home activities, an assessment checklist, and blackline masters for each book pair. This guide has a flexible format that allows teachers to select books and lessons as needed, in a sequence that suits classroom needs and current themes.

AUDIO CASSETTES

There is an audio cassette for each pair of books. The audio cassettes are ideal for reading areas where students can listen to a cassette and read along in their book. These cassettes are useful to students who are on-level readers, at-risk readers, and ESL learners as reinforcement for reading fluency and proficiency. The cassettes allow readers to hear the English language and review troublesome words or text passages. A brief introduction keys the listener into the topic of the book, and the closing asks a question for the listener to think about after hearing the text.

TAKE ME HOME PACKAGES

Individual take-home packages for Emergent Stage 2 help parents get involved in reinforcing reading. Each package includes a pair of books, a bookmark, an audio cassette, and an activity card in English and in Spanish. Stage 2 topics include: apples, seasons, beaches, careers, dinosaurs, and wolves.

TOPICS AND SKILLS CHART

Pair-It Titles	Pair-It Topics	Reading Strategies	Language Skills	Phonics/Word Study
Hushtown: A Peaceful Community and *A Forest Community* pp. 15–20	Communities	• Comprehension: Identifying sequence • Study Skills: Using a glossary	• Recognizing onomatopoeia • Identifying possessive nouns	• Word Study: Identifying compound words • Phonics: Recognizing three sounds of *s*
The Science Fair Surprise and *Think Like a Scientist* pp. 21–26	Scientists	• Genre: Recognizing journal entries • Comprehension: Following steps in a process	• Using quotation marks with dialogue • Understanding specialized language	• Word Study: Recognizing syllables • Word Study: Recognizing noun suffixes
The Amazing Animal Rescue Team and *Fantastic Animal Features* pp. 27–32	Animals	• Comprehension: Recognizing problem/solution • Study Skills: Using photos for information	• Distinguishing common and proper nouns • Using descriptive words	• Phonics: Using hard and soft *c* and *g* sounds • Word Study: Recognizing plurals
The Art Riddle Contest and *Artists and Their Art* pp. 33–38	Art	• Comprehension: Gathering information from text • Genre: Recognizing short biographies	• Recognizing irregular verbs • Distinguishing past and present tense	• Word Study: Identifying inflectional endings *-s, -es, -ed, -ing, -er, -est* • Phonics: Using *r*-controlled vowels *ar, or, er, ir, ur*
Fossils Alive! and *Fossils: Pictures from the Past* pp. 39–44	Fossils	• Genre: Recognizing a fantasy • Comprehension: Drawing conclusions	• Recognizing action verbs • Using irregular plurals	• Word Study: Identifying word roots • Phonics: Recognizing silent consonants *gh, k, w*
The World's Best Dog-Walker and *The World of Dogs* pp. 45–50	Dogs	• Literary: Understanding dialogue • Comprehension: Identifying main idea/details	• Using figurative language • Using helping verbs *has* and *have*	• Word Study: Understanding homonyms • Phonics: Identifying silent consonants
The Secret of the Silver Shoes and *Shoes Through the Ages* pp. 51–56	Shoes	• Literary: Understanding author's purpose • Study Skills: Using text features	• Using contractions • Using synonyms	• Phonics: Identifying *r*-controlled vowels *ar, or, er, ir, ur* • Word Study: Identifying multiple-meaning words

Pair-It Titles	Pair-It Topics	Reading Strategies	Language Skills	Phonics/Word Study
The Mystery of the Missing Leopard and *Wild Cats* pp. 57–62	Wild Cats	• Genre: Recognizing a mystery • Literary: Distinguishing narration from exposition	• Recognizing present tense • Identifying comparatives and superlatives	• Phonics: Identifying *y* as a vowel • Word Study: Identifying syllables in VCCV and VCCCV words
Why the Ocean Is Salty and *Ocean Life: Tide Pool Creatures* pp. 63–68	Oceans	• Genre: Recognizing a pourquoi tale • Study Skills: Interpreting diagrams	• Identifying adjectives • Identifying linking verbs	• Word Study: Understanding words from other languages • Word Study: Identifying compound words
Diary of a Pioneer Boy and *The Pioneer Way* pp. 69–74	Pioneers	• Genre: Recognizing historical fiction • Study Skills: Using parts of a book	• Distinguishing between points of view • Understanding pronouns and antecedents	• Word Study: Recognizing suffixes -*ness*, -*y*, -*ful*, -*ly* • Phonics: Understanding sounds of *air*, *are*, *ear*, *eer*
P.W. Cracker Sees the World and *Our World of Wonders* pp. 75–80	Geography	• Genre: Recognizing humorous fiction • Study Skills: Using maps	• Identifying adverbs • Identifying proper nouns and adjectives	• Phonics: Identifying words with *ew*, *ui*, *au*, *aw*, *al* • Word Study: Recognizing suffixes -*ous*, -*er*, -*or*, -*ist*
Facing the Flood and *Nature's Power* pp. 81–86	Nature's Forces	• Comprehension: Predicting outcomes • Study Skills: Interpreting tables	• Understanding dialogue • Using commas in a series	• Phonics: Identifying the sounds of *oo* • Word Study: Identifying compound words
Casey's Code and *All About Codes* pp. 87–92	Codes	• Literary: Understanding conflicts and resolutions • Comprehension: Applying information	• Identifying adjectives • Understanding acronyms	• Phonics: Identifying syllables with vowels sounded alone • Word Study: Recognizing prefixes *de*-, *in*-, *im*-, *re*-
The Night Queen's Blue Velvet Dress and *The Universe* pp. 93–98	Universe	• Literary: Understanding setting • Study Skills: Using text features	• Understanding compound predicates • Using antonyms	• Phonics: Understanding sounds of *ou* • Word Study: Recognizing suffixes -*en*, -*ous*, -*ion*
Simon's Big Challenge and *Overcoming Challenges: The Life of Charles F. Bolden, Jr.* pp. 99–104	Challenges	• Literary: Understanding character • Genre: Recognizing a biography	• Understanding past tense • Identifying direct quotations	• Phonics: Identifying diphthongs *ow*, *oy*, *oi* • Word Study: Understanding multiple-meaning words

ASSESSMENT

Many opportunities for assessment occur when using *Pair-It Books*. The most valuable assessment tool may be listening to students read and observing how they use the books. Ideas for observations and suggestions for assessment are included in the activities and skill lessons for each pair of books.

Encourage students to self-select titles and notice how they approach the books. Ask them to read the book title and author's name as well as define the topic of the book selected. You may also ask students to tell why they chose that book. Note whether they start with a fiction or a nonfiction title and whether they can tell how the books are different. In order to observe these things, make sure the books are accessible to students. Keep the books in a location where students can easily find them and make selections. Next to the books, you may want to keep a critic's sheet containing a list of the books so students can write comments.

During lesson introductions and before-reading activities, students are asked to tell what they know about a topic and often to predict what they might read about in the book.

Always list, date, and initial student's responses. This will allow them to ask each other questions when working in groups and to verify or change any predictions they may have made about the topic or books. Save this work and refer to it throughout the lesson. These lists and comments can also be used to complete a chart of *What We Know, What We Want to Know,* and *What We Learned.*

Use the *Pair-It Books* Assessment Checklist on pages 109–111 to track students' progress. This evaluation can be included in students' portfolios. The checklist can also be used during conferences with each student. Use the list as a starting point to talk about reading and writing and how students perceive their progress.

The *Pair-It Books* and teacher-modeled classroom writing can serve as a model for students' own writing. Look to see if any of the various patterns and formats in texts are replicated in students' writing. Encourage students to work in pairs to develop stories. Set aside time for students to read their writing aloud. Then you can hear how they are using language, and they can experience sharing their writing with others. The mini lessons provide opportunities to evaluate specific skills students learned as they read the texts.

Also include the work students do in lesson activities and projects as part of an on-going assessment. Additional performance-based assessment can occur as students act out stories, read aloud their writing, give oral reports, create graphs or diagrams, and discuss the books and topics. As students complete projects, it may be helpful to have a project display table. As students explain their projects, listen for demonstrations of learning.

A SAMPLE LESSON

INTRODUCING THE PAIR
The four-page lesson for each pair of books is the instructional core of the *Pair-It Books®* program.

The teacher introduces the topic of a book pair. Students tell what they know about the topic (activating prior knowledge), talk about their relevant personal experiences, and connect their reading of the new books to prior reading.

A synopsis for each book provides a quick reference when selecting titles for introducing books to students.

Why the Ocean Is Salty

Ocean Life: Tide Pool Creatures

The key vocabulary words and glossary words listed can be used for vocabulary development, especially when working with ESL students. The glossary and vocabulary words can be used by students to extend their writing and speaking vocabulary. Students may make a dictionary of words for each book they read. The glossaries at the end of the nonfiction books can help students learn new definitions.

INTRODUCING THE PAIR-IT BOOKS
To introduce the topic of oceans, display the covers of *Why the Ocean Is Salty* and *Ocean Life: Tide Pool Creatures*. Call on a student to read the titles aloud. Ask another student to identify the word that is in both titles. Make a word web on chart paper, writing *ocean* in the center. Invite students to share ideas about oceans. Record their responses on the web.

Why the Ocean Is Salty
The god of the ocean sends his daughters to help the king of Iceland. Locked in the grip of a long winter, his country is starving. The ocean god's daughters use magic millstones to bring spring—and food. The king and others, however, become greedy. The maidens' last gift is a surprise.

Key Vocabulary
bow (ship)	greed	mineral
coast	idle	millstone
conquer	longship	pourquoi
driftwood	maiden	tide

Objectives
Reading Strategy—Genre: Recognizing a pourquoi tale
Language Skill: Identifying adjectives
Phonics/Word Study: Understanding words from other languages

Every book has three stated instructional objectives. For each *Reading Strategy, Language Skill,* and *Phonics/Word Study,* a Mini Lesson targets a specific skill area.

Ocean Life: Tide Pool Creatures
The text, photographs, and diagrams of this book introduce students to the ecology of tide pools, with a special emphasis on the rich variety of animal life in this habitat.

Glossary Words
adapt	high tide	predator
algae	inhabitant	proboscis
bivalve	larvae	scavenger
camouflage	low tide	tentacle
crevice	pincer	

Other Key Vocabulary
barnacle	sea urchin
limpet	tide pool
sea anemone	

Objectives
Reading Strategy—Study Skills: Interpreting diagrams
Language Skill: Identifying linking verbs
Phonics/Word Study: Identifying compound words
For more word study practice, see *Steck-Vaughn Phonics* Level C, Unit 5, pages 125–126.

**Additional Components**
Audio Cassette: *Why the Ocean Is Salty/Ocean Life: Tide Pool Creatures*
Writing Masters, pages 105–108

Other Resources About Oceans
What About Oceans?, Steck-Vaughn
Animals of the Oceans, Stephen Savage
When the Tide Is Low, Sheila Cole
Exploring Water Habitats CD-ROM, Steck-Vaughn

63

The *Additional Components* list tells at a glance what accompanying materials can be used with this lesson.

Audio cassettes are available for use with all the books in Proficiency Stage 5.

Each lesson includes a list of additional books and software on the topic. Many of these books and software are available from *Steck-Vaughn.*

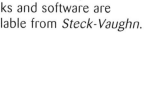

READING THE BOOKS

Before students begin to read, they discuss the book topic and predict what they think the book will be about. You may wish to record and date their responses and save them for use later in the lesson.

Several points of interest about the book are used to help students set a purpose for reading. Questions that promote analysis and critical thinking are provided to guide the reading and to help students frame their thinking as they read.

After reading the book, students follow up on their pre-reading predictions and talk about what they learned. They tell how the book is like or unlike other books they have read on the topic. Children have opportunities to discuss opinions about the book's contents, characters, illustrations, and photos.

Why the Ocean Is Salty

BEFORE READING

Ask students who have visited an ocean to share their ocean experiences. Have them describe the water in the ocean (salty) and ask them to suggest some reasons why the ocean is salty. Write their ideas on the board.

READING

To set a purpose for reading, ask students to read to find out how the maidens on the cover helped the people of Iceland. Use questions such as these to guide the reading:
- *Why is King Ari troubled? (chapter 1)*
- *What things does King Ari want the maidens to do? (chapters 2 and 3)*
- *What things make the maidens unhappy? (chapter 3)*
- *How does greed spoil the happiness of the island people? (chapter 4)*

AFTER READING

Have students compare and contrast the reasons they gave for the ocean's saltiness in Before Reading with the scientific explanation in the introduction and with the explanation in the tale itself.

Writing Activities

Creating a Pourquoi Tale
Materials: audio cassette recorder and audio cassette

Invite groups of students to write their own pourquoi tale. Possible titles include *Why Does the Dog Wag Its Tail?* and *How Did the Skunk Get Its Smell?* Allow groups to read aloud or act out their story for classmates. Some groups may wish to record their story on audio cassette to share with others.

Ocean Song
Materials: chart paper, marker

Lead students in singing "I've Been Working on the Railroad." Then invite students to write new words for the tune that retell all or part of *Why the Ocean Is Salty.* For example, students might begin with the following lines:

We've been waiting for the springtime,
All the live-long day.
We've been waiting for the springtime,
Just to grow some wheat and hay.

64

MINI LESSONS

■ READING STRATEGY

Genre: Recognizing a Pourquoi Tale

Direct students' attention to the word *Why* in the title of the book. Ask students why the ocean is salty, according to the tale. Explain that many pourquoi tales were made up long ago by people who were trying to explain something in nature. Point out that many of the titles start with *Why* or *How.* Share other pourquoi tales, such as *How the Stars Fell into the Sky, How the Guinea Fowl Got Her Spots,* and *Why Mosquitoes Buzz in People's Ears.*

■ LANGUAGE SKILL

Identifying Adjectives

Tell students that an adjective is a word that describes by telling which one, what kind of, how many, or how much. Have students reread the first two sentences on page 4 and identify the adjectives in the sentences. List the adjectives on the board and discuss the question that each one answers.

PHONICS/WORD STUDY

Understanding Words from Other Languages

Reread the introduction on page 3 with students, pointing out that the word *pourquoi* is borrowed from the French language and that it means *why.* Tell students that other French words and phrases, including *café* ("restaurant"), *au gratin* ("with cheese"), and *bon voyage* ("have a good trip") are often used in English. Explain to students the meaning of each.

There are two writing activities for each book in which children provide a personal response to the book in a variety of written formats.

THE MINI LESSONS: READING STRATEGY, LANGUAGE SKILL, AND PHONICS/WORD STUDY

Ocean Life: Tide Pool Creatures

BEFORE READING

Talk with students about what a tide pool is—a pool of seawater left behind when the ocean is pulled away from the shore. Display the cover of the book and point out the starfish and sea anemones. Tell students this book has facts about these and other interesting animals found in tide pools.

READING

To set a purpose for reading, ask students to read to learn more about the animals that live in tide pools. Use questions such as these to guide the reading:
- What is the difference between high tide and low tide? (chapter 1)
- In what ways do tide pool animals protect themselves? (chapters 2–9)
- What do tide pool animals eat? (chapters 2–9)
- What makes life in a tide pool tricky? (chapters 1 and 10)

AFTER READING

On the board write the names of tide pool animals. Have each student choose an animal and say one thing he or she learned about the animal by reading the book.

Writing Activities

Ocean Poetry
Materials: writing or drawing paper, crayons

Invite partners to write a three-line poem about a tide pool creature. Write the following directions and example on the board. Invite partners to illustrate and display their poem.
1. Write the name of the animal.   *Sea scorpion*
2. Write three words that   *Fierce spiny fish*
   tell more about it.   *Spike*
3. Write a nickname for the animal.

Sea Shapes
Materials: construction paper, markers

Invite students to choose an animal from the book, draw its shape on construction paper, and cut out the shape. Have them write facts about the animal on the shape, such as the animal's name and features and what it eats. If possible, provide encyclopedias and nature magazines so students can include additional information on their shape. Display the shapes on a tide pool bulletin board.

MINI LESSONS

■ READING STRATEGY

Study Skills: Interpreting Diagrams

Tell students that a diagram is a picture that shows the parts of something or the order in which something happens. Direct students' attention to the diagram of the crab on page 18. Encourage students to read the diagram in this manner:
1. *Look at the diagram to decide what it shows. If the diagram has a title, read it to help you decide.*
2. *Look at any parts of the diagram.*
3. *Read the labels.*
4. *Think about how all the pieces fit together.*

Then have students look at the diagram of the dog whelk life cycle on page 34 and follow the same steps.

■ LANGUAGE SKILL

Identifying Linking Verbs

Write on the board *A shanny is a fish.* Help students identify the two words that are linked by the verb *is* (*shanny, fish*). Remind students that a linking verb does not show action. It links, or connects, the subject of a sentence to a word in the predicate. Ask students to look in the book to find some linking verbs and the words they link. For example, in the first paragraph on page 3, the linking verb *is* appears three times.

PHONICS/WORD STUDY

Identifying Compound Words

Write the word *seashell* on the board. Ask a student to identify the two words that make up this compound word (*sea, shell*). Then ask students to brainstorm compound words that have the word *sea* or *fish* in them (*seawater, seabird, seaweed, starfish, jellyfish, pipefish, clingfish*).

65

The mini lessons develop and reinforce the comprehension strategies, recognition of genre, literary components, study skills, language skills, phonics, and word study objectives listed in the skills chart on pages 8–9. These lessons can be used for directed reading instruction. The *Writing Masters* and *Assessment Checklist* on pages 105–111 may be used with these mini lessons.

The **Reading Strategy** mini lesson focuses on reading comprehension, genre recognition, literary components, and study skills. Students learn to identify reading strategies, such as main idea and details, plot, setting, or genre. Structural text elements are also the focus of the mini lessons. Structured text, such as diagrams, charts, time lines, and maps are identified and discussed.

The **Language Skill** mini lesson focuses on formats, types of words used in context, structural formats, usage, and grammar. These lessons help students recognize the different ways and patterns in which language is used, as well as how a word changes in spelling according to its use within the text.

The **Phonics/Word Study** feature identifies phonic elements used in the text, which help children learn phonics skills in context. It also identifies word study skills such as compounds, inflectional endings, plurals, and word origins. These brief activities provide opportunities to reinforce and extend skills previously introduced.

TYING THE PAIR TOGETHER

Tying the Pair Together

Display the two books and ask students to compare and contrast them. Ask students to share other information they know about oceans, including information about the plants and animals that live in the ocean, people who live near oceans and the kind of work they do, and ships that travel on the oceans.

Finally, the two books in the pair are tied together. Students tell about the new information they have learned. They can also tell how the two books compare and contrast.

These four activities are cross-curricular. Many include writing activities to encourage language development. Icons indicate whether an activity is recommended for an individual, a pair of students, or a group of students.

Science: Creature Features
Materials: 3 index cards per group

Give each group three index cards and ask students to write one characteristic of a tide pool creature on each card. Groups should exchange cards and write on the reverse side of each the names of the creatures with that characteristic. Discuss students' responses with them and have them make revisions as needed.

Social Studies: Oceans of the World
Materials: globe or physical world map

Display a globe or world map and guide students in exploring the locations of the oceans and seas. Then invite groups to play What's My Name? Begin by giving the clue *I am a sea between New Guinea and Australia* and demonstrating how to locate the Coral Sea. Have groups continue the game on their own. Group members should take turns giving clues.

Language Arts: A Class Yarn
Materials: 40 pieces of yarn, each about 10" long

Wind the yarn into a ball, one piece at a time. Tell students that they are going to make up a class yarn, or story, about the ocean and that each student will have a turn to tell a part of the story. Demonstrate how to unwind one piece of yarn as you begin the story with a few sentences such as *One day Pat decided to take his dog King for a walk near the ocean. He wondered what treasures he might find.* When you reach the end of the first piece of yarn, hand the ball to a student, who should continue the story.

Creative Arts: Tide Pool Habitat
Materials: mural paper, crayons, aprons, diluted blue watercolor paint, large paintbrushes

Divide a long sheet of mural paper in half vertically and add the labels *High Tide* and *Low Tide.* Have students draw tide pools on each half. Then have students paint the *High Tide* half with diluted blue watercolor. The crayons should resist the paint and give that part of the mural an underwater effect.

ASSESSMENT

- Ask students to summarize their reading by naming and describing some animals that live in tide pools and by retelling the explanation for the ocean's salty water in *Why the Ocean Is Salty.*
- Observe whether students can recognize a pourquoi tale in literature that you share with them.
- Display a simple labeled diagram and ask students to tell about it. You might draw the underside of a starfish and label the mouth, arms, eyespots, and tube feet.
- Review samples of students' writings to assess comprehension of what they read.
- Use informal conferencing with students to assess comprehension and skill growth. For further assessment see the checklist on pages 109–111.

Home Activities

Copy and distribute to students the Take It Home activity master on page 67 (English) or on page 68 (Spanish). Invite students to retell the story *Why the Ocean Is Salty* to family members.

66

The assessment suggestions provide ideas for student observations of progress and readiness for standardized tests. They can be used in conjunction with the checklist found on pages 109–111 of this guide. Also see page 10 for ways to use the *Pair-It Books®* for other means of assessment.

Each lesson is followed by a reproducible *Take It Home* activity letter, provided in English and Spanish.

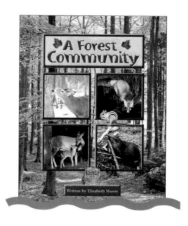

INTRODUCING THE PAIR-IT BOOKS

To introduce the topic of community, display the books *Hushtown: A Peaceful Community* and *A Forest Community*. Ask students to read the titles aloud, then invite students to identify the word that is in both titles. On chart paper, make a word web from *Community*. Have students share ideas about communities as you record their responses on the web.

Hushtown: A Peaceful Community

Two children move to a new town to discover a strange community, where no one is allowed to make loud sounds. This makes it hard for people to talk or have fun or work together. The children start a project that changes the community's feelings about sound.

Key Vocabulary

bullhorn	electrician	noisy
carpenter	factory	official
citizens	hush	peaceful
community	mechanic	pulley
editorial	neighbor	racket

Objectives

Reading Strategy—Comprehension:
   Identifying sequence
Language Skill: Recognizing onomatopoeia
Phonics/Word Study: Identifying compound words
For more word study practice, see *Steck-Vaughn Phonics* Level C, Unit 5, pages 125–126.

Additional Components:

Audio Cassette: *Hushtown: A Peaceful Community/A Forest Community*
Writing Masters, pages 105–108
Take Me Home package

A Forest Community

This book explains how plants and animals interact in the temperate forest community. The book emphasizes plant and animal interdependence.

Glossary Words

burrow	hibernate	microscopic
colony	incisors	predator
communicate	kit	prey
community	larvae	temperate
excavate	lodge	territory
herd		

Other Key Vocabulary

chamber	hollow	sensitive
enemies	pellet	unique
graze	section (verb)	

Objectives

Reading Strategy—Study Skills:
Using a glossary
Language Skill: Identifying possessive nouns
Phonics/Word Study: Recognizing three sounds of *s*
For more phonics practice, see *Steck-Vaughn Phonics* Book C, Unit 1, pages 15–16.

Other Resources About Communities

Aurora Means Dawn, Scott Russell Sanders
Deep in the Rain Forest, Savior Pirotta, Steck-Vaughn
Animals in Their World CD-ROM, Steck-Vaughn

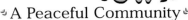

Hushtown
A Peaceful Community

BEFORE READING

Have students look at the cover of the book and ask a volunteer to read aloud the title. Ask a student what *hush* means. Then invite students to predict what the fictional community called *Hushtown* is like. Write their predictions on the board.

READING

To set a purpose for reading, ask students to think about how the main characters feel as they try to adjust to the new community.

Use questions such as these to guide the reading:
- *What clues tell you that Hushtown is different? (chapter 1)*
- *What is Erin and Brian's plan? (chapter 2)*
- *How did the people in the community respond? (chapters 3–5)*
- *How did Erin and Brian change Hushtown? (chapters 5–6)*

AFTER READING

Discuss the predictions students made in *Before Reading.* Then draw a Venn diagram on the board. Ask students how their community is similar to and different from the Hushtown community. Write their responses on the diagram.

Writing Activities

Noisy Names
Materials: crayons, markers, drawing paper

Ask students what they notice about the names of all the people of Hushtown. *(The names are related to sound.)* Have students page through the story and list all the names. Then have students make up other sound names. Ask students to create and illustrate a noisy tale using names from their list.

Rhyme Time
Materials: chart paper, marker

Have groups brainstorm a list of rhyming words that tell about their community, such as *lake/bake, trees/breeze, sun/fun, park/bark.* Invite them to use their rhyming words to write a poem about their community, such as the following:

Our Community

Lots of fun,	*Dogs that bark,*	*Many trees,*	*Big, blue lake*
Plenty sun,	*Flowery park,*	*Soft, clean breeze,*	*Dads that bake*

MINI LESSONS

■ READING STRATEGY

Comprehension: Identifying Sequence

Have students look through the book to identify the steps that Erin and Brian followed to make their tree house. Ask questions such as *What did they do first?* and *What did they do next?* Write the steps on the board. Discuss situations where doing the steps in the right order is important. (*getting dressed, cooking, doing a science experiment*) Then have students write the steps they follow to go swimming or plant a garden.

■ LANGUAGE SKILL

Recognizing Onomatopoeia

Explain that writers sometimes choose words, such as *buzz* or *crash*, that help the reader hear the sounds of the story. These words actually imitate sounds associated with the words or actions they take. Have students look through the book to find examples of these types of words, such as *whisper, bang, whack, smack, bam, slam.*

PHONICS/WORD STUDY

Identifying Compound Words

Write *Hushtown* on the board and have a volunteer read the word aloud. Explain that this word is made up of two words, *Hush* and *town*, that are joined together to make one compound word, *Hushtown.* Invite students to look in the book for other compound words. Students may find such words as *sometimes, grandfather, earmuffs, earplugs,* or *headphones.*

BEFORE READING

Read the title aloud. Remind students that in nonfiction books, important information can be found in pictures, diagrams, charts, and captions. Then write *forest community* on the board, and ask students to think of words that come to mind when they think of a *forest community*. Write their ideas on the board.

READING

To set a purpose for reading, ask students to read to find out where in the forest different animals live.

Use questions such as these to guide the reading:

- *Who lives in a temperate forest community?*
  (chapters 1–6)
- *What do forest animals eat? (chapters 2–6)*
- *At what time of year are young animals seen? (chapters 2–5)*
- *How do the plants and animals help each other in the temperate forest community? (chapters 1–6)*
- *How are people part of the temperate forest community? (chapter 7)*

AFTER READING

Return to the list of words made in Before Reading. Invite students to add other ideas. Write their ideas on the board. Then have pairs write a sentence explaining the definition of *forest community*.

Writing Activities

Forest Fold-Ups
Materials: Strips of drawing paper 5 1/2″× 16″, ruler, colored pencils, encyclopedias

Ask students to make their own books about a forest animal. Provide reference materials so students can discover new facts. Have students fold the paper strip into four equal parts, accordion-style. On the first page, students should draw a picture of the animal. On the other pages, students should write and illustrate facts about the animal.

Connected Community
Materials: none

Write *Animals, Places to Live,* and *Food* as columns on the board. Have students provide information for each column. Invite students to write their responses on the board. Name an animal from the first column and invite students, one at a time to relate any other word or phrase on the board to the animal.

■ READING STRATEGY
Study Skills: Using a Glossary

Point out the word *prey* on page 13 of the book. Ask students what the word means and how they know. Explain that words in dark type are in the back of the book along with a definition. Tell students that such a list is called a *glossary*. Then have partners take turns choosing a word in dark type, predicting the word's meaning, and looking it up in the glossary to confirm their predictions.

■ LANGUAGE SKILL
Identifying Possessive Nouns

Write *owl's wing* and *birds' wings* on the board. Point out that the apostrophe and letter *s* show ownership. Explain that when the apostrophe is before the *s*, the owner is singular, and when it comes after the *s*, the owner is plural. Challenge partners to look through *A Forest Community* to find examples of possessive nouns. Have students tell whether the possessives are singular or plural.

PHONICS/WORD STUDY

Recognizing Three Sounds of *s*

Write the words *house, sure,* and *regions* on the board and circle the letter *s* in each word. Explain that the letter *s* can stand for three sounds: the *s* sound as in *house*, the *sh* sound as in *sure*, and the *z* sound as in *beans*. Invite partners to list words with the three sounds of *s*. Encourage students to look through *A Forest Community* and other books to find *s* words and then to share their lists with other pairs.

Tying the Pair Together

Display the two books. Invite students to compare and contrast the two stories. Use questions such as *How are the communities alike and different? Which community seems like a better place for animals to live? Why? How did the happenings in the communities affect its members?* Create a diagram on the board to show how the communities are alike and different. Fill in the diagram with student ideas.

Social Studies: A Great Place to Visit!
Materials: drawing paper; colored pencils; community resources such as maps, brochures, leaflets, phone book

Have groups make travel brochures about their community by folding the paper into three sections. Encourage students to include facts about places, important people, population size, fun things to do and see—anything to make travelers want to visit the community.

Art: Comic Strip Community
Materials: drawing paper divided into a six-grid, colored pencils, markers, comic strips/books

Provide comic books or comic strips from newspapers that show characters working together. Then ask partners to create a comic strip about how two or more characters work together in a community. The characters can be people or animals.

Geography: Mapping Forest Communities
Materials: encyclopedias, world map, bulletin board, push pins, writing paper, pencils

Invite students to contribute to a bulletin board about temperate forests. Staple a world map to a bulletin board. Point out the different areas that are temperate forests. Then assign each group a temperate forest to research. Have students use push pins and labels to identify their forest on the map. Then have them write a report, identifying the people, plants, and animals that are found there.

Music: Forest Friends Forever
Materials: chart paper, marker

Invite students to write a community song to the tune of "My Bonnie Lies Over the Ocean." Sing the following verse about a forest community to get them started:
The forest is full of creatures,
The forest is full of trees,
The forest is full of creatures,
And they are all friends to me!
Then write down and sing the students' verses.

ASSESSMENT

- Ask students to summarize their reading. They should retell the story of how Hushtown changed and describe animals that live in a temperate forest.
- Ask students to put the events of a book in the correct sequence.
- Observe whether students use the glossary to find the meanings of words they don't know.
- Review samples of students' writings to assess comprehension of what they read.
- Use informal conferencing with students to assess comprehension and skill growth.

For further assessment see the checklist on pages 109–111.

Home Activities

Copy and distribute to students the *Take It Home* activity master on page 19 (English) or on page 20 (Spanish). Invite students to explain how people and animals in communities depend on each other.

TAKE IT HOME

Dear Family of _____,

COMMUNITY ACTIVITIES

Your child has been reading about the communities of animals and people. *Hushtown: A Peaceful Community* is a story about two children who teach their new neighbors about having fun, making noise, and working together. The information book, *A Forest Community*, tells how the animals in a temperate forest depend on each other to live. Choose from the activities below to help your child learn more about communities.

BOOKS ABOUT COMMUNITIES

Help your child learn more about communities by visiting the library. Encourage your child to read and check out the books *It Takes a Village* by Jane Cowen-Fletcher, *Stellaluna* by Janell Cannon, and *The Village Basket Weaver* by Jonathan London.

MOVIES AND MORE

View movies with your child that show animals in forest communities, such as *Bambi* or *The Jungle Book*.

You may also want to listen to the audio cassette *"We Are All America's Children"* by Ella Jenkins to help your child learn about different communities of people.

ARTS AND CRAFTS: Community Diorama

Materials: shoe box, scissors, tempera paint, twigs, aluminum foil

With your child, brainstorm ways people in your neighborhood or community make it a good place to live. Then create a shoebox display to illustrate one idea, such as recycling or planting a community garden. Have your child use tempera paints to paint a background for this scene. Add cardboard or toy people, animals, cars, buildings, twig trees, and a foil pond.

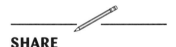

SHARE

Take your child on a walk around your neighborhood and community. Talk about the different people, jobs, shops, homes, and animals that you see on your walk. When you return, invite your child to draw a picture of your community or a map of your neighborhood. Invite your child to tell how the members of a community work together to make it a nice place to live.

Estimada familia de _____,

ACTIVIDADES DE COMUNIDADES

Su niño/a ha estado leyendo acerca de las comunidades de animales y personas. *Hushtown: A Peaceful Community* es la historia de dos niños que le enseñan a sus nuevos vecinos a divertirse, a hacer ruido y a trabajar juntos. El libro de información, *A Forest Community*, cuenta cómo los animales en un bosque temperado dependen unos de otros para vivir. Escoja de las actividades que siguen para ayudar a su niño/a a aprender más acerca de las comunidades.

LIBROS SOBRE COMUNIDADES

Visite la bibioteca para ayudar a su niño/a a aprender más acerca de las comunidades. Anime a su niño/a a leer y a sacar los libros *It Takes a Village* por Jane Cowen-Fletcher, *Stellaluna* por Janell Cannon y *The Village Basket Weaver* por Jonathan London.

PELÍCULAS Y MÁS

Vea películas con su niño/a que muestran animales en comunidades en bosques, tales como *Bambi* o *The Jungle Book*.

También pueden escuchar el casete *"We Are All America's Children"* por Ella Jenkins para ayudar a su niño/a a aprender sobre diferentes comunidades de personas.

ARTE Y ARTESANÍA: Diorama de la comunidad

Materiales: caja de zapatos, tijeras, pintura a témpera, ramitas, papel de aluminio

Genere ideas con su niño/a sobre las formas en que la gente de su vecindario trabaja para hacerlo un buen lugar para vivir. Después usen la caja de zapatos para hacer una demonstración e ilustrar una idea, como el reciclar o plantar un jardín para la comunidad. Pida a su niño/a que use pintura a témpera para colorear un fondo para la escena. Agreguen gente de cartón o de juguete, animales, automóviles, árboles de ramitas y una laguna de papel de aluminio.

COMPARTAN

Lleve a su niño/a a un paseo alrededor del vecindario y la comunidad. Conversen acerca de las diferentes personas, trabajos, tiendas, casas y animales que vean en el paseo. Cuando regresen, invite a su niño/a a hacer un dibujo de la comunidad o del vecindario. Invite a su niño/a a contar cómo los miembros de una comunidad trabajan juntos para hacerla un lugar agradable para vivir.

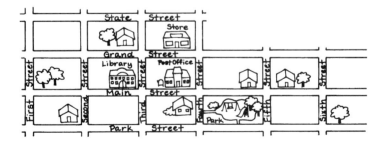

INTRODUCING THE PAIR-IT BOOKS

To introduce the topic of science and scientists, display the books *The Science Fair Surprise* and *Think Like a Scientist.* Have students read the titles and compare the covers. On chart paper, make a two-column chart with *science* and *scientists* as headings. Invite students to share ideas about each of these words as you record their responses.

The Science Fair Surprise

Katy Beth Allen wants to create the most surprising science fair project ever. She plans to make a volcano, but another student chooses this idea first. Katy Beth finally comes up with an idea that amazes everyone.

Key Vocabulary

assembly	kaleidoscope	reflect
erupt	larvae	tattoo
evaporation	lava	transparent
experiment	microscope	volcano
geyser	project	

Objectives

Reading Strategy—Genre: Recognizing journal entries

Language Skill: Using quotation marks with dialogue

Phonics/Word Study: Recognizing syllables

For more word study practice, see *Steck-Vaughn Phonics* Level C, Unit 5, pages 135–152.

Think Like a Scientist

Think Like a Scientist describes six fields of science and the work scientists do in these fields. Experiments and a flow chart of the scientific method are also included.

Glossary Words

astronomer	geologist	oceanographer
chemical	hypothesis	physicist
chemist	light-year	result
current	matter	satellite
experiment	meteorologist	scientific method

Other Key Vocabulary

data	forecast	telescope
discoveries	resources	pollution

Objectives

Reading Strategy—Comprehension: Following steps in a process

Language Skill: Understanding specialized language

Phonics/Word Study: Recognizing noun suffixes

For more word study practice, see *Steck-Vaughn Phonics* Level C, Unit 6, pages 169–170.

Additional Components

Audio Cassette: *The Science Fair Surprise/ Think Like a Scientist*

Writing Masters, pages 105–108

Take Me Home package

Other Resources About Science

Everyday Science, Michael H. Gabb

Electricity, Janice VanCleave

Interactive Science Encyclopedia CD-ROM, Steck-Vaughn

The SCIENCE FAIR Surprise

BEFORE READING

Invite students to tell about science projects they have seen or made for a science fair. Discuss any group projects the students may have participated in. Then ask them to name the most surprising projects they have seen. List them on the board.

READING

To set a purpose for reading, ask students to read to find out if Katy Beth creates an amazing science project.

Use questions such as these to guide the reading:

- *How does Katy Beth's idea for a science project change? (chapters 1–5)*
- *What happenings in the story help Katy Beth develop her science project? (chapters 1–5)*
- *How does Katy Beth feel about her new project on water? (chapter 3)*
- *What does she write about in her journal? (chapters 3, 4)*
- *What is Katy Beth's true wonder of Water World? (chapter 5)*

AFTER READING

Ask if students would have been surprised by Katy Beth's wonder of Water World. *Why? Why not?* Then invite students to share how they thought Katy Beth felt.

Writing Activities

Wonder of Water Flow Chart
Materials: colored pencils, drawing paper

Remind students that Katy Beth presented her project in several steps. Ask students to scan pages 30–32 to find out the sequence of events. Then invite students to write and illustrate a flow chart showing the sequence of her presentation. Invite them to take turns acting out the presentation using their flow chart.

Great Scientists Discussion
Materials: encyclopedias

Brainstorm with students a list of different kinds of scientists. Review with students some of the important qualities scientists need, such as curiosity, good math skills, and good organization. Choose a kind of scientist and have students research three more qualities that this kind of scientist needs. Ask partners to write a short paragraph about scientists' qualities and why they are needed.

■ READING STRATEGY
Genre: Recognizing Journal Entries

Explain that a journal is a written record of what happens to someone or what someone thinks. Have students find and reread some of Katy Beth's journal entries. Ask students to keep a science journal for a week. At the end of the week invite students to share their journals with other students.

■ LANGUAGE SKILL
Using Quotation Marks with Dialogue

Direct students' attention to the first sentence on page 4 of the book and read it aloud. Then point out the quotation marks, and explain that these punctuation marks show a speaker's exact words. Ask who is speaking in this sentence (*Maya*), and what are the first and last words of her statement (*I, today*). Tell students that the beginning quotation marks appear before the first word in the quote, and the ending marks appear after the last word in the quote. Have volunteers read aloud quotes from the book.

PHONICS/WORD STUDY

Recognizing Syllables

Remind students that a *syllable* is a word or word part with only one vowel sound. Write *surprise* and *fair* on the board, and help volunteers identify which word has one syllable and which has two. Tell students that they can listen for the number of vowel sounds in a word to determine the number of syllables. Read aloud words from the book and have students hold up one finger for words with one syllable and two fingers for words with two syllables.

Think Like a Scientist

BEFORE READING

Ask students to read aloud the title of the book. Point out the key word *Scientist*. Then create a word map on the board with *Scientists* in the center. Write the words and phrases *jobs, fields, how they work,* and *safety rules* around the center. Invite students to provide additional information for the map.

READING

To set a purpose for reading, ask students to read to find out about six different fields of science.

Use questions such as these to guide the reading:
- *Why do scientists perform experiments? (chapter 1)*
- *How does the work scientists do affect other people? (chapters 1–7)*
- *How do scientists go about doing a study or experiment? (chapter 1)*
- *What do scientists try to predict or discover? (chapters 2–7)*

AFTER READING

Return to the word map made in Before Reading. Invite students to add other ideas from the book. Ask volunteers to take turns naming a field of science and describing the work of scientists in that field.

Writing Activities

Scientific Thinking
Materials: materials for conducting experiments listed in the book, drawing or chart paper

Invite groups to choose one or more of the experiments in the book. Then with adult supervision, help the groups conduct the experiments following the scientific method. Have students record their experiment. Ask students to divide the paper into fourths and label the sections in order with these steps: *1. Question, 2. Hypothesis, 3. Experiment, 4. Results.* Encourage students who conducted the same experiments to compare their results.

The Night the Lights Went Out
Materials: none

Remind students that electricity is one important force that physicists study. Have students shut their eyes and imagine that one evening all the electricity in the world has gone out. Then have partners talk to each other about what they think might happen. You may also ask partners to write a story entitled "The Night the Lights Went Out."

■ READING STRATEGY
Comprehension: Following Steps in a Process

Direct attention to page 8, and have students look at the steps for the experiment. Ask *What is the first step? What is next?* Explain that doing the steps in order make the end result successful. Discuss the steps in making a peanut butter and jelly sandwich. Write the steps on the board. Then ask students what might happen if the steps were done out of order.

■ LANGUAGE SKILL
Understanding Specialized Language

Write the words *astronomy, chemistry,* and *satellite* on the board. Explain that nonfiction books often have words that are special to a particular topic. Read the words on the board aloud and point out that these words have special meanings in the field of science. Tell students that when they come to unfamiliar specialized words in their reading, they may be able to figure out the meanings by reading the rest of the paragraph. Students may also use the glossary or a dictionary to find out what a specialized word means.

PHONICS/WORD STUDY

Recognizing Noun Suffixes

Explain that a *suffix* is a word part added to the end of a base word that changes its meaning. Write *-er, -or,* and *-ist* on the board and explain that these suffixes mean "a person who." Write *scientist* on the board and ask students what this means *(a person who studies science)*. Challenge students to think of other words with suffixes *-er, -or,* and *-ist.* Write their responses on the board.

Tying the Pair Together

Display the two books and ask students to tell how the books are alike and different. Invite volunteers to tell what they learned about science. Then have students write one or two sentences about an interesting part of each book. Allow them to refer to the books as needed.

Social Studies: Who Am I?
Materials: None

Have students take turns pretending to be scientists. Give students clues about different scientists to share with group members. Have students read the scientist clues aloud so group members can guess their jobs. For example, one student might give the clue "I study resources such as gems and oil." (*geologist*)

Math: Experimenting with Shadows
Materials: tape measure, chalk, drawing paper, marker

Help partners measure each other's shadow in the morning, at noon, and in the afternoon of a sunny day. Have them take turns tracing each other's shadow and measuring the length of the drawing. Encourage partners to make a chart to show their measurements.

Science: Weather Watchers
Materials: outdoor thermometer, weather vane, rain gauge (optional)

Help students set up weather monitoring equipment in an outdoor area. If you don't want to use a purchased weather vane, you can hang a strip of fabric from a tree limb or observe a school flag. Have students note the time and weather data two or three times per day for a week. At the end of the week discuss how the weather changed from day to day or from one time of day to another.

Science: Chemical Mix-Ups
Materials: water, oil, vinegar, salt, drink powder, sand, soil, clear plastic container with tight-fitting lid, goggles

Invite students to discover which materials mix with water and which ones do not. Before assisting students with the mixing, have them make predictions. Help students pour water into the container, add a material, replace the lid, and shake the container. Observe what happens and chart the results. To ensure students' safety have them wear goggles and clean up spills immediately. Remind students not to taste any of the materials.

ASSESSMENT

- Ask students to describe several areas of science that were in the fiction and nonfiction books.
- Observe whether students can follow steps in a process and give reasons for doing so.
- Display a thank-you note for students to compare and contrast to a journal entry.
- Review samples of students' writings to assess comprehension of what they read.
- Use informal conferencing with students to assess comprehension and skill growth.

For further assessment see the checklist on pages 109–111.

Home Activities

Copy and distribute to students the *Take It Home* activity master on page 25 (English) or page 26 (Spanish). Invite students to talk about the work scientists do in their community.

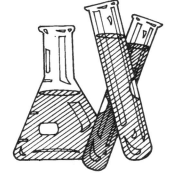

Dear Family of _____,

SCIENCE ACTIVITIES

Your child has been reading about science and scientists. *The Science Fair Surprise* is an imaginative story about a clever girl who wants to create the most surprising science fair project ever. The information book, *Think Like a Scientist*, describes six different fields of science. To help your child learn more about science and scientists, choose from the activities below.

BOOKS ABOUT SCIENCE

Help your child learn more about science by visiting the library. Invite your child to check out books such as *Day Light, Night Light: Where Light Comes From* by Franklyn M. Branley and *The Rattlebang Picnic* by Margaret Mahy.

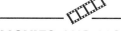

MOVIES AND MORE

To encourage your child's interest in science, together watch the public television programs *Bill Nye, the Science Guy* and *Newton's Apple*. Then with your child try some of the simple science experiments discussed on the public television programs.

ARTS AND CRAFTS: Tornado Safety Rules

Materials: drawing paper, crayons, pencil

Discuss with your child that meteorologists study weather. Explain that a tornado is a dangerous kind of weather. Then talk about what to do during a tornado watch or warning. Remind your child that it is best to seek shelter in a basement if possible. If that's not possible, take shelter in the most central part of a building. Tell your child that next it is important to lie on the floor and cover up with a blanket or pillow. After the discussion, ask your child to create a safety rules poster to follow during a tornado watch or warning.

SHARE

Explore the science of chemistry with your child by cooking a food, such as biscuits, pancakes, or a cake. As the food cooks, discuss how chemicals such as baking powder or soda and milk react to make the food rise.

Tornado Safety Rules
1. Seek shelter in the basement or in the center of the building.
2. Lie down.
3. Cover up with a blanket or pillow.

Estimada familia de _____ ,

ACTIVIDADES DE CIENCIAS

Su niño/a ha estado leyendo sobre ciencias y científicos. *The Science Fair Surprise* es un cuento imaginativo acerca de una niña habilosa que quiere crear el proyecto más sorprendente que se haya hecho para la feria de ciencias. El libro de información, *Think Like a Scientist*, describe seis diferentes ramas de la ciencia. Escoja de las actividades que siguen para ayudar a su niño/a a aprender más sobre ciencias y los científicos.

LIBROS DE CIENCIAS

Visite la biblioteca para ayudar a su niño/a a aprender más sobre ciencias. Invite a su niño a sacar libros tales como *Day Light, Night Light: Where Light Comes From* por Franklyn M. Branley y *The Rattlebang Picnic* por Margaret Mahy.

PELÍCULAS Y MÁS

Para animar a su niño/a a interesarse por las ciencias, miren juntos los programas de la televisión pública *Bill Nye, the Science Guy* y *Newton's Apple*. Luego, con su niño/a, prueben hacer algunos de los experimentos simples mencionados en los programas de la televisión pública.

ARTE Y ARTESANÍA: Reglas de seguridad con los tornados

Materiales: papel de dibujo, creyones, lápiz

Converse con su niño/a sobre los meteorólogos que estudian el tiempo. Explique que un tornado es una condición del tiempo muy peligrosa. Luego hablen sobre lo que hay que hacer cuando se anuncia la posibilidad de un tornado o cuando se ha visto un tornado. Recuerde a su niño/a que lo mejor es buscar refugio en un subterráneo o sótano si es posible. Si no es posible, hay que buscar refugio en la parte central de un edificio. Dígale que es importante tenderse en el suelo y cubrirse con una frazada o almohada. Después de la conversación, pídale que haga un cartel con las reglas de seguridad que hay que seguir durante la posibilidad de un tornado.

COMPARTAN

Explore la ciencia de la química con su niño/a preparando un alimento, tal como pancitos, panqueques o un pastel. Mientras se cuece el alimento, conversen acerca de cómo las sustancias químicas como los polvos de hornear o el bicarbonato y la leche reaccionan y sirven para levadura en los alimentos.

Tornado Safety Rules
1. Seek shelter in the basement or in the center of the building.
2. Lie down.
3. Cover up with a blanket or pillow.

INTRODUCING THE PAIR-IT BOOKS

Introduce the topic of animals and their special features by displaying copies of *The Amazing Animal Rescue Team* and *Fantastic Animal Features*. Discuss the titles and identify the first book as realistic fiction and the second as nonfiction. Activate students' knowledge of wild animals by brainstorming a list of animals that live in these habitats: forest, jungle, ocean, and mountains.

The Amazing Animal Rescue Team

Three young members of the World Animal Rescue Team spend the summer helping troubled wild animals. The team travels to Australia, Madagascar, and Borneo. Maps at the beginning of each chapter help readers to locate the places the team visits.

Key Vocabulary

continent	equipment	released
defense system	laptop computer	signaling
e-mail	nature preserve	spelunking
endangered	primate	

Objectives

Reading Strategy—Comprehension:
Recognizing problem/solution
Language Skill: Distinguishing common and proper nouns
Phonics/Word Study: Using hard and soft *c* and *g* sounds
For more phonics practice, see *Steck-Vaughn Phonics* Level C, Unit 1, pages 13–14.

Fantastic Animal Features

What young bird has claws in its wings? *Fantastic Animal Features* has the answer. The book teaches readers about the special features of some unusual animals.

Glossary Words

angler	environment	prey
aquatic	habitat	primates
arboreal	nocturnal	semiaquatic
camouflage	pectoral fins	spiny
coral	predator	venomous
dorsal fins		

Other Key Vocabulary

ability	mammals	odor
features	nubs	

Objectives

Reading Strategy—Study Skills: Using photos for information
Language Skill: Using descriptive words
Phonics/Word Study: Recognizing plurals
For more word study practice, see *Steck-Vaughn Phonics* Level C, Unit 5, pages 153–154.

Additional Components

Audio Cassette: *The Amazing Animal Rescue Team/ Fantastic Animal Features*
Writing Masters, pages 105–108

Other Resources About Animals

Eyewitness Funfax: Weird and Wonderful, Susan Mayes and Andrew Peters
Backyard Rescue, Hope Ryden
Animals in their World CD-ROM, Steck-Vaughn

THE Amazing Animal RESCUE TEAM

BEFORE READING

Discuss the book title and cover, and then ask students to listen as you read aloud the first paragraph on page 3 and all of page 5. Have students predict how the team will help with the wallaby "invasion." Then read the table of contents together to preview the team's other assignments.

READING

To set a purpose for reading the book, ask students to think about a time when animals might need help from humans. Also encourage students to read to find out how the World Animal Rescue Team provides help to animals.

Use questions such as these to guide the reading:

- *How do the animals respond to being rescued? (chapters 2–4)*
- *Why is it important for the team to help the animals? (chapters 2–4)*
- *What are some of the techniques the team uses in its rescues? (chapters 2–4)*
- *How do the team members work together? (chapters 2–4)*

AFTER READING

Form three groups of students and assign a book episode to each one. Have group members reread their episode. Then have them describe their animal's natural habitat, tell why it was in trouble, and explain how the World Animal Rescue Team helped.

Writing Activities

Writing an Assignment
Materials: multiple copies of *The Amazing Animal Rescue Team*

Review the rescue team's assignments on pages 5, 13, 21, and 32. Help students to research other animals that live in areas the team visited (*Australia, Madagascar, Borneo, Texas*). Have students write their own animal rescue assignments describing the animal's name, its location, its problem, and the solution.

Animal Stories
Materials: drawing paper, markers, crayons

Initiate a discussion about students' own adventures with animals. Invite them to develop oral stories about the episodes. Encourage students to illustrate a part of the story for the audience.

■ READING STRATEGY

Comprehension: Recognizing Problem/Solution

Explain that there are three main problems in the book, and that each is described in an assignment. Have a volunteer read page 5. Then ask students how the team solved the problem. Help them to understand that problems and solutions can have several parts. Then discuss the problems on pages 13 and 21. Students can then brainstorm solutions for the problem on page 32.

■ LANGUAGE SKILL

Distinguishing Common and Proper Nouns

Remind students that nouns name people, places, things, and ideas. Then write on the board *Borneo is an island in the Pacific.* Call on volunteers to identify the nouns in the sentence. Explain that *Borneo* and *Pacific* are proper nouns and capitalized because they name specific places. Tell students that *island* is a common noun because it names a general place. Ask volunteers to write additional examples on the board.

PHONICS/WORD STUDY

Using Hard and Soft *c* and *g* Sounds

Write these words on the board: *Africa, fence, rescue, continent, bounce,* and *receive.* Have students read the words aloud. Underline the letter *c* in each one. Read aloud *Africa, rescue,* and *continent;* explain that in these words the *c* has a hard sound. Read aloud *fence, bounce,* and *receive;* explain that in these words the *c* has a soft sound. Repeat for hard and soft *g,* using these words: *tiger, huge, endanger, guide, gently,* and *vegetable.*

Fantastic ANIMAL FEATURES

BEFORE READING

Discuss the book title and cover of *Fantastic Animal Features*. Then page through the book with students and make a list of the types of animals included. Ask students to create a chart with these headings: *What We Know, What We Want to Know,* and *What We Learned.* Have students write their ideas in the first two columns.

READING

To set a purpose for reading, ask students to read to find out what makes each of the animals unique.

Use questions such as these to guide the reading:
- *How do some of the animals use camouflage? (chapters 2–9)*
- *What are some of the animals' special features that help them survive in their habitats? (chapters 2–9)*
- *How are some of the young animals different from their parents? (chapters 3, 7, 9)*
- *How do the animals' abilities change to help them survive in their environments? (chapters 2–3)*

AFTER READING

Have students add more animal facts to the third column of their charts, indicating what they learned.

Writing Activities

Picture Captions
Materials: drawing paper, colored pencils

Invite students to select a favorite animal from *Fantastic Animal Features*. Have them make a detailed drawing of the animal in the center of the paper. Then help students label several of the animal features. Invite students to write to explain how each feature helps the animal survive.

Listening/Writing Time
Materials: literature about animals

To expand students' interest and knowledge about animals, read aloud 15 minutes each day from literature about animals. Try these books: *The Reason for the Pelican* by John Ciardi (poems); *Hawk, I'm Your Brother* by Byrd Baylor (short story in verse); or *The Cat Who Came for Christmas* by Cleveland Armory (longer story). Allow for class discussion following the readings. After a week of oral reading time, work with students to write a class book about animal features or abilities.

MINI LESSONS

■ READING STRATEGY

Study Skills: Using Photos for Information

Model for students how to get information from a photo. Refer to the photo of the frogfish on page 6 and state the information it gives about the creature's physical appearance, special features, abilities, or habitat. Then read aloud the pages in the book that describe the animal and discuss how the photo adds to those facts.

■ LANGUAGE SKILL

Using Descriptive Words

On the board print *Toads have bumpy, dry skin and shorter legs.* Call on a volunteer to read the sentence aloud. Point to *skin* and *legs.* Explain that the adjectives *bumpy* and *dry* describe *skin.* Call on a volunteer to find another adjective in the sentence. Then print this sentence on the board: *Basilisks like humid and hot weather.* Ask students to find adjectives that describe *weather.*

PHONICS/WORD STUDY

Recognizing Plurals

Review the terms *singular* and *plural,* and then write on the board *frog, branch, calf, baby, foot,* and *fish.* Read the words aloud and explain that each is singular. Ask volunteers for the plural forms. Then have students compare the two forms. Lead students to conclude that some plurals are formed by adding *-s,* but that words that end with *ch* add *-es.* Point out that when *baby* becomes plural the *y* changes to *i* and that when *calf* becomes plural the *f* changes to *v* and *-es* is added. Explain that *foot* has an irregular plural and *fish* is singular and plural.

Tying the Pair Together

Display the two books. Call on volunteers to compare the two books. Then distribute index cards and divide the class into three groups. Have the first group make a name card for each animal in the books. Ask the second group to list special features, and the third group to list special abilities. Then call on volunteers from each group to place the cards with the book that reflects what was learned.

Science: Animal Observations
Materials: none

Have individual students observe an animal (a pet or a local wild animal) for 15 minutes. Ask students to record their observations. How does it move? What does it eat? How does it protect itself? Then have students compare their observations.

Geography: Where in the World?
Materials: globe or world map, self-stick notes, encyclopedias, wildlife magazines

Groups of students can learn geography by finding the home continent for the animals described in the two books. Give each group one or two animal names to research. Have the groups write animal names on self-stick notes. Then help the groups place their animal names on each animal's home continent.

Mathematics: Fast Animals
Materials: information books about land animals, colored pencils, drawing paper

Create a simple bar graph comparing the sprinting speed of the cheetah (nearly 70 miles per hour—see page 4 of *The Amazing Animal Rescue Team*) to that of the common house cat (30 miles per hour). Review the graph with students. Then instruct students to research other animals' speeds. Have pairs of students present their information by drawing and writing the name of each animal on the left side of a chart and creating a horizontal bar to indicate the distance each animal can travel per hour.

Arts: Crafty Camouflage
Materials: posterboard, markers, crayons

Organize the class into groups of four and take a walk outdoors, stopping occasionally to allow students to observe areas where insects might live. Upon return, have each group create a poster of an insect environment with three to five camouflaged insects. Swap the posters with other groups to see if they can locate the camouflaged insects.

ASSESSMENT

- Ask students to summarize a part in each book. They should describe an animal rescue as well as one unusual animal feature and its purpose.
- Observe whether students can identify the problems and solutions in a book.
- Display a detailed photograph and have students tell you as much as they can about it.
- Review samples of students' writings to assess comprehension of what they read.
- Use informal conferencing with students to assess comprehension and skill growth.

For further assessment see the checklist on pages 109–111.

Home Activities

Copy and distribute to students the *Take It Home* activity master on page 31 (English) or on page 32 (Spanish). Invite students to discuss with their families the facts they have learned about animals' features.

TAKE IT HOME

Dear Family of _____,

ANIMAL ACTIVITIES

Your child has been studying about some very unusual animals. Your child has also been reading *The Amazing Animal Rescue Team*, a story about young animal rescuers. The information book, *Fantastic Animal Features*, tells about amazing animals and their features. To help your child learn more about animals, try some of the activities below.

BOOKS ABOUT ANIMALS

Help your child learn more about animals by visiting the library. Look for the monthly magazine, *Ranger Rick*, published by the National Wildlife Federation. Also encourage your child to check out these two, fact-filled easy readers: *Big Cats* and *Wild, Wild Wolves* by Joyce Milton.

MOVIES AND MORE

With your child, find videos about amazing animals at your local library and video rental store. *Balto* is based on the true story of an Alaskan sled dog. National Geographic's *Deep Sea Dive* shows real footage of ocean life. Be sure to watch the award-winning film *Babe*, which is about a special pig.

ARTS AND CRAFTS: Amazing Animal Photo Book

Materials: discarded nature magazines, art paper, glue stick, scissors, stapler

Work with your child to make an amazing animal photo book. Look through nature magazines and cut out pictures of animals. Talk about the animals' special features as you glue down the pictures on art paper. Combine the papers to make an art book.

SHARE

Animals are everywhere. Help your child learn more about the animals living near his or her home. For one week, keep a record of the animals you and your child see. Post a sheet on the refrigerator to record your sightings. Talk about the list at the end of the week.

LLÉVAME A CASA

Estimada familia de _____,

ACTIVIDADES DE ANIMALES

Su niño/a ha estado estudiando acerca de algunos animales poco comunes. Su niño/a también ha estado leyendo *The Amazing Animal Rescue Team*, un cuento acerca de unos jóvenes rescatadores de animales. El libro de información, *Fantastic Animal Features*, cuenta acerca de animales sorprendentes y sus características. Pruebe algunas de las actividades que siguen a continuación para ayudar a su niño/a a aprender más acerca de los animales.

LIBROS SOBRE ANIMALES

Visite la biblioteca para ayudar a su niño/a a aprender más acerca de los animales. Busque la revista mensual, *Ranger Rick*, publicada por la National Wildlife Federation. Además anime a su niño/a a sacar prestado estos dos libros llenos de información y de fácil lectura: *Big Cats* y *Wild, Wild Wolves* por Joyce Milton.

ARTE Y ARTESANÍA: Un asombroso libro de fotos de animales

Materiales: revistas viejas sobre naturaleza, papel de arte, barra adhesiva, tijeras, grapadora

Trabaje con su niño/a para hacer un libro de fotos de animales asombrosos. Busquen en las revistas de naturaleza y recorten dibujos de animales. Hablen sobre los rasgos especiales que tengan los animales mientras los pegan en el papel de arte. Combinen los papeles para formar un libro de arte.

PELÍCULAS Y MÁS

Con su niño/a, busque videos sobre animales asombrosos en la biblioteca local y en la tienda para alquilar videos. *Balto* está basado en una historia verídica acerca de un perro para trineos de Alaska. *Deep Sea Dive* de la National Geographic muestra secuencias reales sobre la vida marina. Asegúrese de ver *Babe*, la película que ganó un premio, que trata sobre un cerdo especial.

COMPARTAN

Hay animales por todas partes. Ayude a su niño/a a aprender más sobre los animales que viven cerca de su casa. Anoten los animales que Usted y su niño/a vean durante una semana. Pongan una hoja en el refrigerador para anotar lo que vayan viendo. Conversen sobre la lista al final de la semana.

INTRODUCING THE PAIR-IT BOOKS

Read aloud the titles of the two books. Explain that *The Art Riddle Contest* is about a class trip to an art museum where students see the works of famous artists. By contrast, *Artists and Their Art* gives short biographies of the same artists. To activate students' knowledge, brainstorm two lists together: *Materials Artists Use* and *What Artists Create*.

The Art Riddle Contest

Mrs. Lee motivates her students for a trip to the art museum. She gives partners riddles to solve and announces that she has art sets for the partners who correctly solve the riddles. That's all the motivation aspiring-artists Stacy Morgan and Inky Nelson need to make the best of the field trip.

Key Vocabulary

acrylic	fabric	sculptor
charcoal pencil	gallery	sculptures
chisel	massive	technique
contest	murals	unique
expression	museum	

Objectives

Reading Strategy—Comprehension: Gathering information from text

Language Skill: Recognizing irregular verbs

Phonics/Word Study: Identifying inflectional endings –s, -es, -ed, -ing, -er, -est

For more word study practice, see *Steck-Vaughn Phonics* Level C, Unit 5, pages 129–130.

Artists and Their Art

This book is a collection of short biographies that explore the lives and work of six major artists. All were artistic children and pursued their love of art into adulthood.

Glossary Words

artistic	inspire	scenic
cubism	landscape	sculptor
determined	masterpiece	sculpture
encourage	Mestizo	studio
express	mural	tradition
fabric		

Other Key Vocabulary

academy	gallery	style

Objectives

Reading Strategy—Genre: Recognizing short biographies

Language Skill: Distinguishing past and present tense

Phonics/Word Study: Using *r*-controlled vowels *ar, or, er, ir, ur*

For more phonics practice, see *Steck-Vaughn Phonics* Level C, Unit 4, pages 93–94.

Additional Components

Audio Cassette: *The Art Riddle Contest/Artists and Their Art*

Writing Masters, pages 105–108

Other Resources About Art

Diego Rivera, Steck-Vaughn
Tar Beach, Faith Ringgold

The Art Riddle Contest

BEFORE READING

Help your students become familiar with riddles. Give your students some simple riddles to solve, such as *What is black and white and read all over?* (newspaper) Then explain to students that *The Art Riddle Contest* has riddles about art.

READING

Encourage students to set a purpose for reading. Suggest that students read to find out what the art riddles are and who wins the contest.
Use questions such as these to guide the reading:

- *How do Mrs. Lee's clues and riddles help her students to appreciate the art museum? (chapters 1–6)*
- *How does Stacy help Inky overcome his shyness? (chapters 2–6)*
- *What are some materials that artists used to create the art in the museum? (chapters 3–6)*
- *Which artists' work shows the Southwest? (chapter 4)*

AFTER READING

Ask students to look again at the artwork in the book. Have each student select a favorite and write down three reasons for their choice. Then have students discuss the artwork they chose.

Writing Activities

Track a Friendship
Materials: self-stick notes, copies of *The Art Riddle Contest*

An important theme in the book is the friendship that develops between Stacy and Inky. The author includes several exchanges between the two that indicate this development. Have students work in groups to locate and tag excerpts that show these exchanges. Afterward, have volunteers read the excerpts in book order. Discuss how students can use similar techniques in their own writing. Then have groups write a short story in which a friendship between two characters develops.

Art Expression
Materials: colored pencils or markers, drawing paper

Explain to students that artists use their art to express thoughts, experiences, and feelings. Then tell students that writers and poets do the same type of expression with words. Have students think of something they'd like to express to others such as a thought or feeling. Then ask students to write a short paragraph or poem to express it. Invite students to illustrate their writing.

▪ READING STRATEGY

Comprehension: Gathering Information from Text

Remind students to read for clues about what's important in the story. Read aloud page 3 and point out the ways in which the author lets readers know that Stacy and Inky will be the main characters. Then read aloud page 7 and call on volunteers to tell how the last paragraph alerts us to what Stacy might do. *(help Inky get more involved)*

▪ LANGUAGE SKILL

Recognizing Irregular Verbs

Print on the board these two sentence starters, *Today Stacy . . .* and *Yesterday she . . . .* Under them, list these regular present- and past-tense verbs: *learns, learned* and *talks, talked* and point out the *-s* and *-ed* endings. Ask students to read the resulting sentence pairs. Then add to the list irregular verbs such as *eats, ate; runs, ran;* and *wins, won.* Point out that the past tense verbs do not have *-ed* endings; instead the words change. Explain that when the words change the verbs are called "irregular."

PHONICS/WORD STUDY

Identifying Inflectional Endings *-s, -es, -ed, -ing, -er, -est*

Write the following sentence on the board: *By mixing yellow and red paints, the artist made the brightest orange he'd ever seen.* Underline *mix, paint,* and *bright.* Read the sentence aloud and point out the base words and endings. Afterward, model for students how to add endings to words. Then have volunteers use the words with endings in a sentence.

Artists and Their Art

BEFORE READING

Copy each glossary word on an index card and distribute the cards to students. Then write *artist* on the board. Have students read aloud their word. Explain that the words all relate to artists or art as you write them on the board under *artist*. Ask students to brainstorm other words that are related to *artist* and *art*.

READING

To set a purpose for reading, ask students to read to discover what the six artists were like when they were young. Use questions such as these to guide the reading:

- *What subject matter did the six artists depict in their work? (chapters 1–6)*
- *Which of the artists were influenced by African art? (chapters 2, 4, 5)*
- *What or who encouraged the artists in the book to create their art? (chapters 1–6)*
- *What is the style of each artist? (chapters 1–6)*

AFTER READING

Print the names of the six artists across the board and have students recall and reread passages from the book about each artist's childhood. Have volunteers summarize the information and write it below the names. When the chart is complete, call on volunteers to use the information to note similarities and differences in the artists' backgrounds.

Writing Activities

Critique an Artwork
Materials: copies of *Artists and Their Art*

Have each student study a favorite piece of art in the book. Ask students to write two or three paragraphs telling how the artist's life influenced what the work depicts and what techniques and materials he or she used in the work.

Gallery Guide
Materials: fine art magazines or postcards

Provide each student in a small group with a photograph of artwork from a magazine or postcard. If possible, the artwork for each group should have a common feature, such as the artist, medium, creation date, or geographic region in which the work was created. Help each student write a paragraph about his or her piece of art. Then have each group present a tour of their "gallery" to the other groups.

MINI LESSONS

■ READING STRATEGY

Genre: Recognizing Short Biographies

Explain that a biography is the story of a person's life. It tells when and where the person was born and what he or she did throughout parts or all of his or her life. Read aloud a few anecdotes to show how the author brings the artists to life in *Artists and Their Art*. Read, for example, about the experiences in Faith Ringgold's life that inspired the creation of *Tar Beach*.

■ LANGUAGE SKILL

Distinguishing Past and Present Tense

Tell students that verbs are words that express action or a state of being. Then read these sentences aloud and discuss how the verbs tell when something happens: *Amado Peña liked to copy comic books. (past) Peña paints in bold bright colors with strong lines. (present)* Then invite volunteers to make up sentences using present and past tense verbs.

PHONICS/WORD STUDY

Using *r*-Controlled Vowels *ar, or, er, ir, ur*

Explain that when *r* follows a vowel, the vowel sound is neither long nor short. Read aloud the following words with the vowels *a* or *o*: *can, art, paint, hard, same, sharp, had; bold, born, show, soft, for, long, horse.* Next, read aloud words with the vowels *e, i,* or *u*: *purse, his, squirt, he, like, fun, girl, best, time, burn, left, just, child, fern.* Help students to hear the sounds of the letter pairs *er, or, ar, ir,* and *ur*.

Tying the Pair Together

Remind students that *The Art Riddle Contest* and *Artists and Their Art* show the work of great artists. Locate other books that show other works by the six artists from the books, or by other famous artists. Divide the class into six groups and assign each group an artist. Have each group select two pieces of the artist's work. Then help each group make up riddles about the work. Have students use the riddles and the artwork in a contest.

Geography: Learn from Landscapes
Materials: drawing paper, chalk, watercolor paints and brushes, scissors, glue, assorted scraps of paper, magazines

Have students create a painting, drawing, or collage showing a place he or she would like to visit. Have students share their artwork with each other and guess where each other's landscape may be. Combine the landscapes into a class book.

Writing: We're All Artists
Materials: drawing paper, colored pencils, markers

Have students make a group drawing. One student begins the artwork by drawing a line or a shape on the paper. As the paper is passed around the classroom each student adds a line or a shape. When each student has contributed, display the finished art. Ask students to create a title for the piece and to write a paragraph about what it was like to create the artwork. Invite students to share their writings and discuss each student's interpretation of the experience.

Art: Inspired Creations
Materials: assorted art materials

Have students create art inspired by one of the six artists featured in the books. Begin by talking about the artist's techniques and subject matter. Students can work alone, in pairs, or as a class on one large piece.

Writing: Art Experts
Materials: large index cards, colored pencils

Invite students to make a game that tests their knowledge of art and artists. Have small groups write on separate index cards six questions such as *What large artwork is painted directly on a wall?* or *I make soft sculptures like rag dolls. Who am I?* Groups should exchange cards and spend a few minutes finding the answers. Then as a class, discuss the questions and answers.

ASSESSMENT

- Have students select one of the featured artists and tell about his or her life and work.
- Ask students to describe the strategies they use to retain information during or after reading.
- Ask students to list four kinds of information they could find in a short biography.
- Review samples of students' writing to assess comprehension of what they've read.
- Use informal conferencing with students to assess comprehension and skill growth.

For further assessment see the checklist on pages 109-111.

Home Activities

Copy and distribute to students the *Take It Home* activity master on page 37 (English) or page 38 (Spanish). Invite students to discuss with their families the understanding they have gained about art and artists.

 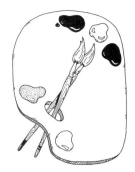

Dear Family of _____,

ART ACTIVITIES

Your child has been reading about art and artists. The information book, *Artists and Their Art*, is about these six artists: Amado Peña, Faith Ringgold, Georgia O'Keeffe, Hale Woodruff, Pablo Picasso, and Elisabet Ney. *The Art Riddle Contest* is a story about a class that visits a museum and uses clues to find art by some of the same artists.

ART BOOKS

With your child, visit the library and check out these books about artists: *Deep Blues: Bill Traylor, Self-Taught Artist* by Mary E. Lyons, and *Artist in Overalls: The Life of Grant Wood* by John Duggleby. If your child wants to try some art projects, check out *My First Paint Book* by Dawn Sirett.

MOVIES AND MORE

With your child, view movies and videos about art and artists. *Linnea in Monet's Garden* is an animated film about a young girl's fascination with the work of a French artist. *The Boy Who Drew Cats* tells the story of a Japanese boy who must find his own way in life. Talk with your child about subjects, colors, and sizes of the art in these movies.

ARTS AND CRAFTS: Colorful Collage

Materials: old greeting cards and postcards, magazine pictures, colored papers, glue, scissors, cardboard

Help your child gather an interesting collection of colored papers and pictures. You might want to look for pictures in magazines about one subject. As you cut the pictures and papers into smaller pieces, talk about ways to arrange them. Then on a large piece of cardboard, glue down the colorful pieces to create a collage.

SHARE

Artists see the world in a special way because they look at things very carefully. Try this exercise together to discover how an artist might look at things. With your child, look at a scene such as a playground. Take turns saying what you see. Try to make at least two statements about what you see, such as *I see the shadow outline of the whole swing set. I see a long pole across the top.*

Copyright © Steck-Vaughn Company

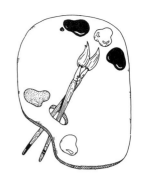

LLÉVAME A CASA

Estimada familia de _____,

ACTIVIDADES DE ARTE

Su niño/a ha estado leyendo acerca de arte y artistas. El libro de información, *Artists and Their Art*, trata sobre estos seis artistas: Amado Peña, Faith Ringgold, Georgia O'Keeffe, Hale Woodruff, Pablo Picasso y Elisabet Ney. *The Art Riddle Contest* es un cuento acerca de una clase de estudiantes que visita un museo y usa pistas para buscar arte por los mismos artistas.

LIBROS DE ARTE

Con su niño/a, visite la biblioteca y saque prestado estos libros sobre artistas: *Deep Blues: Bill Traylor, Self-Taught Artist* por Mary E. Lyons y *Artist in Overalls: The Life of Grant Wood* por John Duggleby. Si su niño/a quisiera ensayar con algunos proyectos de arte, saque *My First Paint Book* por Dawn Sirett.

PELÍCULAS Y MÁS

Vea películas y videos sobre arte y artistas con su niño/a. *Linnea in Monet's Garden* es una película animada acerca de la fascinación de una joven por el trabajo de un artista francés. *The Boy Who Drew Cats* narra la historia de un niño japonés quien necesita buscar su propio camino en la vida. Converse con su niño/a sobre los temas, colores y tamaños del arte en estas películas.

ARTE Y ARTESANÍA: Collage de vivos colores

Materiales: tarjetas de felicitaciones y postales viejas, fotos de revistas, papel de colores, goma de pegar, tijeras, cartulina

Ayude a su niño/a a reunir una interesante colección de papeles de colores y fotos. Puede que quieran buscar fotos en revistas sobre un tema. Mientras cortan las fotos y papeles en pedazos más pequeños, conversen sobre maneras de organizarlos. Luego en un pedazo grande de cartulina, peguen los pedazos de colores vivos para formar un collage.

COMPARTAN

Los artistas ven el mundo de manera especial porque miran las cosas cuidadosamente. Hagan este ejercicio juntos para descubrir cómo un artista mira las cosas. Con su niño/a, miren una escena tal como el patio de recreo. Tomen turnos para contar lo que vean. Traten de decir por lo menos dos declaraciones sobre lo que vean, tales como: *Yo veo la silueta de todo el juego de columpios. Yo veo un poste largo sobre la parte de encima.*

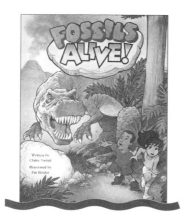

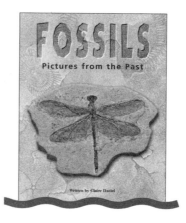

INTRODUCING THE PAIR-IT BOOKS

Display the two books and call on a student to read aloud the titles. Explain that *Fossils Alive!* is a fantasy about a class trip to a science museum and that *Fossils: Pictures from the Past* offers facts about fossils. To activate students' knowledge about fossils, develop a word web. Write *Fossils* on the board. Ask students to tell what they know about fossils. Record the responses.

Fossils Alive!

Alli and Robert go with their class to the Interactive Science Museum, and the two are surprised to discover just how interactive it is! A special time-travel booth sends them to the Jurassic Period, where they are nearly crushed by a hungry Allosaurus.

Key Vocabulary

Allosaurus	evaporates	remains
amble	exhibit	Stegosaurus
Apatosaurus	fossil	volcano
cast	interactive	Ultrasaurus
decaying	Jurassic Period	
dense	mineral	

Objectives

Reading Strategy—Genre: Recognizing a fantasy
Language Skill: Recognizing action verbs
Phonics/Word Study: Identifying word roots

Fossils: Pictures from the Past

Using text, diagrams, and photos, this book tells how fossils form and how they help paleontologists discover the history of life on Earth. The book also tells about people who find fossils, including eight-year-old Christopher Wolfe who unearthed a fossil belonging to a 90-million-year-old horned dinosaur.

Glossary Words

amber	*Iguanodon*	Triassic Period
embryo	mammoth	*Triceratops*
evaporate	mineral	trowel
extinct	paleontologist	*Tyrannosaurus rex*
fossil	*Proterochampsa*	
growth rings	skeleton	

Objectives

Reading Strategy—Comprehension: Drawing conclusions
Language Skill: Using irregular plurals
Phonics/Word Study: Recognizing silent consonants *gh, k, w*
For more phonics practice, see *Steck-Vaughn Phonics* Level C, Unit 3, pages 83–84.

Additional Components

Audio Cassette: *Fossils Alive!/Fossils: Pictures from the Past*
Writing Masters, pages 105–108
Take Me Home package

Other Resources About Fossils

Jacob Two-Two and the Dinosaur, Mordecai Richler
Trapped in Tar: Fossils from the Ice Age, Caroline Arnold
Message in a Fossil: Uncovering the Past CD-ROM, Steck-Vaughn

BEFORE READING

Have students summarize stories in which characters travel in time, either into the future or back to the past. Have them recall what triggered the travel; perhaps it was a mechanical device, a picture, or a written passage. Finally, refer to a few pictures in *Fossils Alive!* to introduce the characters Robert and Alli.

READING

To set a purpose for reading, suggest that students read to find out how Alli and Robert find the answer to the question, "Was it possible for a Tyrannosaurus rex to kill and eat a Stegosaurus?"

Use questions such as these to guide the reading:

- *What do Alli and Robert learn about fossil formations? (chapters 1–2, 4)*
- *What clues do Robert and Alli find to indicate they have traveled back to dinosaur times? (chapters 3, 4)*
- *What plant and animal fossils did Robert and Alli see on their trip? (chapters 3–5)*
- *How do Alli and Robert find the answer to their assigned question? (chapters 2–4)*

AFTER READING

Call on volunteers to describe the device that triggers Robert and Alli's travel back to the Jurassic Period. Then have students recall the answer that the two found to their assigned question.

Writing Activities

Story Timeline
Materials: None

Invite partners to create a sequence map of the story. To start, have them draw a vertical line about an inch from the left edge of lined paper and mark six or eight, equally-spaced points along it. To the right of each point, have students summarize a main event in the story. Invite students to use the sequence maps to retell the story.

Time-Travel Brochures
Materials: drawing paper, markers or colored pencils, copies of *Fossils Alive!*

Have small groups of students study the illustrations of the time-travel booth in the book. Then, challenge them to make their own time-travel brochure promoting travel to the Jurassic Period. When the brochures are completed, display each group's brochures in the classroom.

■ READING STRATEGY

Genre: Recognizing a Fantasy

Explain that stories that include unrealistic events and characters are called *fantasies*. To reinforce the definition, recall one or two events in the story that are fantasy. Then have students summarize other story events and identify them as realistic or fantasy.

■ LANGUAGE SKILL

Recognizing Action Verbs

Write *pointed, said, flashed, makes, covers, hardens, digs,* and *finds* on the board. Have a student read the words aloud. Explain that these words are action verbs because they tell what something or someone does. Then read aloud the first two paragraphs on page 20 and have students listen for action verbs. Continue to read page 20; challenge students to identify more action verbs.

PHONICS/WORD STUDY

Identifying Word Roots

Tell students that some of the longer words in this book are made up of word parts. Explain that knowing what the parts mean can help you figure out what the word means. Write the roots *dino* and *saurus* on the board. Explain that *dino* is a root word from the Greek word that means "monstrous"; *saurus*, also from a Greek word, meaning "lizard." Then define the roots *Tyranno* ("tyrant") and *Ultra* ("huge") as you write them on the board. Challenge students to add them to *saurus* and give the meaning of the newly formed words.

FOSSILS:
Pictures from the Past

BEFORE READING

To heighten student's interest in the book, give each a slip of paper and have students print one thing that they know about the topic *fossils*. Have a volunteer read the slips of paper aloud in class as you write the information in the first column of a KWL chart. Ask students what they would like to learn about fossils. Write these things on the board in the second column.

READING

Invite students to set a purpose for reading. Ask students to read to find five facts that fossils have taught us about life on Earth long ago.
Use questions such as these to guide the reading:
- *What is a fossil? (chapters 1, 2)*
- *What animals and plants are mentioned in the book? (chapters 1–5)*
- *What can we learn from fossils? (chapters 1–5)*
- *How do people find fossils? (chapters 4–6)*

AFTER READING

Call on volunteers to explain how fossils are created. Then have students tell what they have learned as you list the information in the third column of the KWL chart.

Writing Activities

Information Display
Materials: drawing paper, colored pencils, reference books

Have each student contribute to a display of fossil information. Each student's work should include a paragraph or more, plus a labeled picture, graph, or diagram about a term. Assign these terms: *amber, animal fossil, Iguanodon, mammoth, plant fossil, tree trunk fossil, paleontologist, Proterochampsa, tools for fossil digs, Triassic Period, Triceratops,* and *Tyrannosaurus rex.* Monitor and assist students with their work.

Make a Fossil Book
Materials: construction paper, markers, crayons, copies of *Fossils: Pictures from the Past*

Have students work together in small groups to review chapter 2. Ask students to identify the steps involved in forming a fossil. Then have them write and illustrate a short book explaining these steps. Students can make a cover for the book with construction paper. They should write a title and their name on the cover.

■ READING STRATEGY
Comprehension: Drawing Conclusions

Explain that authors sometimes expect readers to think about what they read and draw conclusions from it. For example, in *Fossils: Pictures from the Past*, the author points out that scientists study fossils to learn about the past, so readers conclude that fossils are important sources of history about life on Earth.

■ LANGUAGE SKILL
Using Irregular Plurals

Remind students of the definitions of *singular* and *plural*. Then print the following nouns on the board, under the heading *Singular: tooth, foot, wolf, leaf,* and *life.* Explain that each word is unusual because we do not add *-s* or *-es* to make it plural. Add the heading *Plural* on the board. Ask volunteers to write the plural forms of the singular words. Discuss the changes in the words and explain that plurals such as these are called "irregular."

PHONICS/WORD STUDY

Recognizing Silent Consonants
gh, k, w

Write the following sentences on the board and have a volunteer read them aloud: *As the dinosaurs fought, they knocked down trees. Wreckage was everywhere.* Underline the *gh* in *fought,* the *k* in *knocked,* and the *W* in *Wreckage.* Explain that these consonants are silent. Afterward, ask students to write words such as *knee, light, know, knife, knob, light, might, sigh, wrist, write,* and *wrong.* Then ask students to underline the silent consonant or consonants in each word.

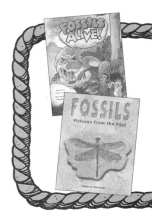

Tying the Pair Together

Display copies of both books. Ask students to compare the information about fossils in each book. Then have students write a story of their own about fossils. Suggest these questions as story themes: *How would you discover a fossil? What would you do next? What would it be like to be a paleontologist?*

Science: Fossil Museum Bulletin Board
Materials: information books, index cards, markers

Have students research to find out about animals, plants, and insects that were alive during the Jurassic Period and that are alive today *(gingko tree, tuatara, cockroach, dragonfly, fish, etc.)*. Then have students write a short paragraph summarizing their findings. Invite them to add illustrations. Display the cards on a Science Fossil Museum bulletin board.

Mathematics: Relative Size Bar Graphs
Materials: information books, markers, encyclopedias, drawing paper

Have students research to find the height or length of several dinosaurs and present-day large animals. Then have students make a bar graph comparing the dinosaurs' and animals' height or length. Students should include a scale such as 1 inch = 1 foot.

Art: Plaster Molds and Casts
Materials: clay, plaster of Paris, small seashells

Explain to students that there are two types of fossils: molds and casts. Then help students make models of both types. Press a small shell into a piece of clay. Explain that this is a mold. Then fill the indentation in the clay with plaster. When the plaster hardens, remove the clay. Explain that the plaster formed a cast.

Drama: Character Presentations
Materials: Pair-It Books about Fossils

Invite interested students to portray the characters and fossil discoverers in *Fossils Alive!* and *Fossils: Pictures from the Past.* Assign these roles: Mrs. Fry, Robert, Alli, Timothy Leland, Mary Ann Mantell, Gideon Mantell, Sir Richard Owen, Martin Lockley, and Christopher Wolfe. Students should review the passages about their "character" and prepare brief oral presentations using the first person to describe him or her.

ASSESSMENT

- Ask students to explain how fossils help us learn about the history of life on Earth.
- As students read aloud, occasionally pause to ask what conclusions they might draw from the reading.
- Have students explain how they know when a story is a fantasy.
- Review samples of students' writing to assess comprehension of what they read.
- Use informal conferencing with students to assess comprehension and skill growth.

For further assessment see the checklist on pages 109-111.

Home Activities

Copy and distribute to students the *Take It Home* activity master on page 43 (English) or page 44 (Spanish). Invite students to discuss at home the facts they have learned about fossils.

TAKE IT HOME

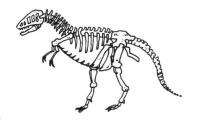

Dear Family of _____,

FOSSIL ACTIVITIES

Your child has been reading about fossils. A book called *Fossils Alive!* tells the story of two school children on a field trip to an interactive science museum. While at the museum, the two children travel back to the time of the dinosaurs. *Fossils: Pictures from the Past* is an information book about how fossils are formed and what they tell us about life on Earth millions of years ago.

FOSSIL BOOKS

You and your child can find more books about fossils and dinosaurs by visiting the library. Here are two information books to check out: *Dinosaurs Walked Here and Other Stories Fossils Tell* by Patricia Lauber and *Discover Dinosaurs: Become a Dinosaur Detective* by Chris McGowan.

ARTS AND CRAFTS: Make a Fossil

Materials: modeling clay, small objects

Tell your child that some fossils are the remains of living things, such as bones and teeth. Other fossils are imprints made by plants and animals. Help your child make "instant fossils" by flattening balls of clay and pressing shells or sturdy leaves into them.

MOVIES AND MORE

With your child, view movies or videos about dinosaurs and fossils. *Dinosaurs, The Flesh on the Bones* shows how fossils are used to unravel the mystery of the dinosaurs. *Dinosaurs and Other Creature Features* from National Geographic connects dinosaurs to their living relatives.

SHARE

From fossils, scientists have learned about life in the time of dinosaurs. Imagine that 50 million years from now scientists are studying about our lives based on a few common objects. With your child, select some objects and talk about what scientists would learn.

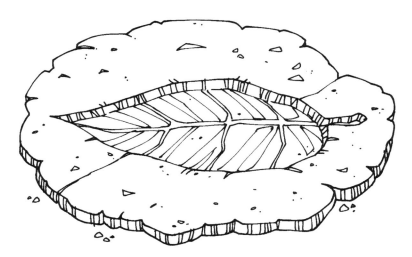

LLÉVAME A CASA

Estimada familia de _____,

ACTIVIDADES DE FÓSILES

Su niño/a ha estado leyendo acerca de fósiles. Un libro llamado *Fossils Alive!* cuenta la historia de dos escolares que van al museo interactivo de ciencias. Mientras están en el museo, los dos niños retroceden en el tiempo hasta la época de los dinosaurios. *Fossils: Pictures from the Past* es un libro de información sobre cómo se forman los fósiles y lo que nos cuentan sobre la vida sobre la Tierra hace millones de años atrás.

LIBROS DE FÓSILES

Usted y su niño/a pueden encontrar más libros sobre fósiles yendo a la biblioteca. Pueden sacar prestado estos dos libros de información: *Dinosaurs Walked Here and Other Stories Fossils Tell* por Patricia Lauber y *Discover Dinosaurs: Become a Dinosaur Detective* por Chris McGowan.

ARTE Y ARTESANÍA: Hagan un fósil

Materiales: arcilla, objectos pequeños

Cuéntele a su niño/a que algunos fósiles son los restos de cosas vivas, tales como huesos y dientes. Otros fósiles son impresiones hechas por plantas y animales. Ayúdele a su niño/a a hacer "fósiles instantáneos" por aplastando bolitas de arcilla y presionando conchitas u hojas firmes contra ellas.

PELÍCULAS Y MÁS

Vea películas o videos acerca de dinosaurios y fósiles con su niño/a. *Dinosaurs, The Flesh on the Bones* muestra cómo se usan los fósiles para desenmarañar el misterio de los dinosaurios. *Dinosaurs and Other Creature Features* de la National Geographic conecta a los dinosaurios con sus parientes vivientes.

COMPARTAN

Los científicos han aprendido acerca de la época de los dinosaurios a través de los fósiles. Imagínense que en 50 millones de años los científicos estarán estudiando nuestras vidas usando unos pocos objetos comunes. Con su niño/a, seleccione algunos objetos y hablen sobre lo que aprenderían los científicos.

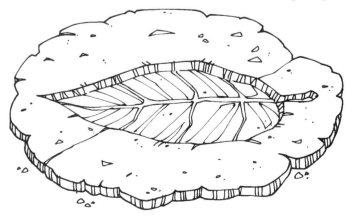

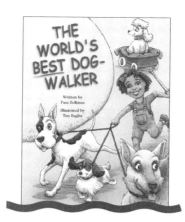
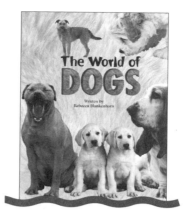

INTRODUCING THE PAIR-IT BOOKS

To introduce the topic of dogs, display the covers of *The World's Best Dog-Walker* and *The World of Dogs* and have volunteers read the titles aloud. Ask students to share their experiences with dogs. Then ask them to name different kinds of dogs, such as collie, beagle, German shepherd, and golden retriever.

The World's Best Dog-Walker

In this humorous and heart-warming story, Abby starts a dog-walking business in her neighborhood. Her best friend, Bird, says she wants no part of it but repeatedly comes to Abby's aid. By helping Abby, Bird becomes comfortable with dogs. At the end of the story, Bird joins Abby in business.

Key Vocabulary

allergic	gigantic	quiver
cocker spaniel	Great Dane	rhinestone
finicky	leash	sheepishly
frustrated	poodle	
German shepherd	pug	

Objectives

Reading Strategy—Literary: Understanding dialogue
Language Skill: Using figurative language
Phonics/Word Study: Understanding homonyms
For more word study practice, see *Steck-Vaughn Phonics* Level C, Unit 7, pages 195–196.

Additional Components

Audio Cassette: *The World's Best Dog-Walker/ The World of Dogs*
Writing Masters, pages 105–108

The World of Dogs

This nonfiction book introduces the many breeds of dogs, from the tiny Chihuahua to the huge Irish wolfhound. It also features a history of the dog and describes other members of the canine family.

Glossary Words

ancestor	domesticated	purebred
breed	habitat	rodent
canine	pack	scavenger
carnivore	prehistoric	social
distraction	prey	

Other Key Vocabulary

cooperate	stray
fetch	mutt
herd	retrieve

Objectives

Reading Strategy—Comprehension: Identifying main idea/details
Language Skill: Using helping verbs *has* and *have*
Phonics/Word Study: Identifying silent consonants
For more phonics practice, see *Steck-Vaughn Phonics* Level C, Unit 3, pages 83–84.

Other Resources About Dogs

Pet Riddles and Jokes with Franny and Frank, Steck-Vaughn
The Call of the Wild, Jack London
Animals in Our World CD-ROM, Steck-Vaughn

THE WORLD'S BEST DOG-WALKER

BEFORE READING

Ask students to think of jobs young people often have, such as babysitting and yard work. Brainstorm with students problems that young people can face in those jobs. Then display the book cover and have students read the title of the book. Ask students to predict what problems a dog-walker might face. Write the predictions on the board.

READING

To set a purpose for reading, ask students to read to find out unusual ways to walk a dog. Use questions such as these to guide the reading:

- *What ideas for earning money do Abby and Bird have? (chapter 1)*
- *Why does Bird refuse to join the dog-walking business? (chapter 2)*
- *Why is Fifi called Finicky Fifi? (chapter 4)*
- *What things make Abby and Bird "perfect partners"? (chapter 5)*

AFTER READING

Have students compare their Before Reading predictions with the dog-walking problems Abby has. Then ask students how Abby's problems are solved.

Writing Activities

Business Flyer
Materials: drawing paper, colored pencils

Invite groups of students to imagine they are starting their own business. Ask them to come up with a kind of business and a name for it. Then have students design an advertising flyer for their business. Encourage students to use language that will make their business as attractive as possible. Display the flyers around the room.

Dog Debate
Materials: none

Have students decide which kind of dog in the book makes the best pet and write a paragraph explaining their choice. Invite students to read aloud their paragraph. Then have students vote to see which kind of dog most class members think makes the best pet.

■ READING STRATEGY

Literacy: Understanding Dialogue

Explain to students that writers use quotation marks to indicate a speaker's exact words and that a change in speakers is signaled by a new paragraph. Read aloud the first paragraph on page 8 and ask students to identify the speaker (Abby). Have volunteers read the rest of the dialogue on the page and identify the speaker in each paragraph.

■ LANGUAGE SKILL

Using Figurative Language

Have students turn to page 21 and focus on the simile "She raced down the sidewalk like a kid running to the swimming pool on the first day of summer." Point out that in this sentence the writer compares the way Clover runs to the way a child runs to a pool on the first day of summer—that is, eagerly. Ask students to find and explain the comparisons with *like* in paragraph 3 of page 3 and paragraph 1 of page 31. Then help students write a simile of their own. If necessary, provide them with the framework *He walked to school like _____.*

PHONICS/WORD STUDY

Understanding Homonyms

Ask students to find the words *know* and *no* on pages 8 and 12. Explain that *know* and *no* are homonyms, words that sound the same but have different spellings and meanings. Discuss with students the meaning of each word and invite volunteers to use them in sentences. Then have partners look through the book to find other homonyms and use them in sentences.

The World of DOGS

BEFORE READING

Display the cover of *The World of Dogs* and have a volunteer read the title aloud. Brainstorm with students some of the ways in which dogs help people. Write student responses on the board.

READING

To set a purpose for reading, ask students to read to learn about dog breeds that are unfamiliar to them. Use questions such as the following to guide the reading:

- *How are dogs alike and different? (chapter 1)*
- *What things make some dogs good sporting dogs? (chapter 2)*
- *What kinds of work do dogs do now, and what kinds have they done in the past? (chapters 1–4)*
- *What other animals belong to the canine family? (chapter 5)*

AFTER READING

Help students review and expand the list they made in Before Reading. Then ask them to look through the book and add to their list of breeds that are commonly used for each task.

Writing Activities

Comparing and Contrasting Dog Breeds
Materials: colored pencils (optional)

Ask students to choose two dog breeds from the book. Next, have them list the characteristics of each chosen breed. Then, have students write a paragraph comparing or contrasting the two breeds. Students may wish to include drawings that highlight the similarities or differences.

Dog Ditty
Materials: none

Have small groups of students write a three-line poem about a breed of dog. Write the following directions and example on the board. Invite groups to illustrate and display their poem.

1. *Write the name of the breed, followed by <u>dog</u>.*
2. *Write three words to describe the breed, followed by <u>dog</u>.*
3. *Make up a name for the dog, followed by <u>Dog</u>.*

Dachshund dog
Long funny digging dog
Diggity Dog

■ READING STRATEGY

Comprehension: Identifying Main Idea/Details

Explain to students that many paragraphs have a main idea. Have students read the first paragraph on page 12 and identify the main idea, which is stated in the first sentence. Explain that other ideas in the paragraph are details. Then have students read paragraph 2 on page 19 and decide on the main idea (*things police dogs must learn to do*). Have partners take turns reading selected paragraphs to identify the main idea.

■ LANGUAGE SKILL

Using Helping Verbs Has and Have

Remind students that a verb phrase is made up of a main verb and one or more helping verbs. Point out the first sentence on page 25. Explain that *have* is used with plural subjects and *has*, with singular subjects. Ask students to write sentences in which they correctly use the helping verbs *have* and *has*. Students can then exchange sentences and identify the helping verbs.

PHONICS/WORD STUDY

Identifying Silent Consonants

Write the words *light, comb,* and *knot* on the board and read them aloud. Ask students to identify the silent consonants in the words and invite volunteers to offer other words with these silent consonants. Encourage students to look through the book to locate other words with silent *gh, b,* and *k*.

Tying the Pair Together

Display copies of *The World's Best Dog-Walker* and *The World of Dogs*. Ask students to imagine that they have met someone who has never seen a dog and does not know what a dog is. Invite students to define *dog* and to name and describe the different breeds for the person.

Creative Arts: Dog Dream House
Materials: drawing paper, colored pencils or markers

Have students design the perfect dog house. Encourage them to think of what a dog needs and might want in his or her home. Ask students to label each feature.

Social Studies: Dog Dictionary
Materials: 3-hole writing paper, 3-hole folder, colored pencils, markers, encyclopedias, information books about dogs

Ask partners to create an illustrated dog dictionary listing and defining all the dog breeds they learned about. Encourage students to use additional resources to find out about other dog breeds and to include those breeds in their dictionary. Invite students to display their completed work in a folder.

Health/Physical Education: Hot Dog!
Materials: lightweight ball

Organize students into a circle and have them play Hot Dog. Choose one student to stand in the center with a ball. Have this student ask a question about dogs and bounce the ball to another student. If the student correctly answers the question, he or she trades places with the student in the center. If the student cannot answer correctly, he or she bounces the ball back. The student in the center asks the question again and bounces the ball to another student.

Science: Pet-Care Poster
Materials: poster board, markers, resources on dog care (optional)

If possible, provide resources on dog care, such as brochures from a local veterinarian. Or brainstorm guidelines for taking care of a dog. Include information about exercise, water, food, shelter, vaccinations, and grooming. Then ask groups to create a colorful pet-care poster.

ASSESSMENT

- Ask students to summarize their reading. They should describe the appearance and abilities of dogs and retell Abby and Bird's dog-walking experiences.
- Have students identify stated and unstated main ideas in selected paragraphs of nonfiction.
- Ask students to identify the speaker in each paragraph of a passage of dialogue from a fiction book.
- Review samples of students' writings to assess comprehension of what they read.
- Use informal conferencing with students to assess comprehension and skill growth.

For further assessment see the checklist on pages 109–111.

Home Activities

Copy and distribute to students the *Take It Home* activity master on page 49 (English) or page 50 (Spanish). Invite students to share what they learned about dogs with someone at home.

TAKE IT HOME

Dear Family of _____,

DOG ACTIVITIES

Your child has been reading about dogs. *The World's Best Dog-Walker* is a heart-warming story about a girl who starts up a dog-walking business in her neighborhood. The companion book, *The World of Dogs*, includes characteristics of many different breeds of dogs. To help your child learn more about dogs, choose from the activities below.

DOG BOOKS

Help your child learn more about dogs by visiting the library. Mark Evans' book *ASPCA Pet Book for Kids: Puppy* tells how to take care of a new puppy. An inspiring reading experience awaits your child in *The Bravest Dog Ever: The True Story of Balto* by Natalie Standiford.

MOVIES AND MORE

Spend an afternoon with your child watching a dog movie, such as *Air Bud, Homeward Bound: The Incredible Journey,* or *Old Yeller*. Discuss the relationships between the dog(s) and the people in the movie. You may also want to discuss the challenges that the dog(s) or people face in the movie.

ARTS AND CRAFTS: A Dog's View

Materials: unlined paper, pencil, crayons or markers

Fold four sheets of paper together to make a booklet. Then with your child write a story about a dog from the dog's point of view. You may want to write about a dog you know or retell a familiar story about a dog. Illustrate the story and then invite your child to share it with other family members and friends.

SHARE

If possible, visit a pet shop or animal shelter with your child to look at different kinds of dogs. Encourage your child to ask the shopkeeper or the attendant about the different breeds and needs of the dogs.

LLÉVAME A CASA

Estimada familia de _____,

ACTIVIDADES DE PERROS

Su niño/a ha estado leyendo acerca de perros. *The World's Best Dog-Walker* es un cuento enternecedor acerca de una niña que comienza un negocio paseando perros en su vecindario. El libro compañero, *The World of Dogs*, incluye características de diversas razas de perros. Para ayudarle a su niño/a a aprender más sobre perros, escoja de las actividades que siguen.

LIBROS DE PERROS

Usted y su niño/a pueden aprender más sobre perros yendo a la biblioteca. El libro por Mark Evans *ASPCA Pet Book for Kids: Puppy* cuenta como cuidar a un cachorrito. Una inspiradora experiencia de lectura le espera a su niño/a cuando lea *The Bravest Dog Ever: The True Story of Balto* por Natalie Standiford.

PELÍCULAS Y MÁS

Pase una tarde con su niño/a viendo una película de perros, tales como *Air Bud, Homeward Bound: The Incredible Journey* u *Old Yeller*. Conversen sobre la relación entre los perros y la gente en la película. Puede que también quieran conversar sobre los desafíos que los perros o la gente enfrentan en la película.

ARTE Y ARTESANÍA: El punto de vista de un perro

Materiales: papel sin líneas, lápiz, creyones o marcadores

Doblen cuatro hojas de papel para hacer un folleto. Luego escriba un cuento con su niño/a acerca de un perro desde el punto de vista del animal. Puede que quieran escribir acerca de algún perro que conozcan o volver a contar algún cuento conocido acerca de un perro. Ilustren el cuento y luego invite a su niño/a a que comparta el cuento con otros miembros de la familia o amistades.

COMPARTAN

Si es posible, visite una tienda de mascotas o refugio para animales con su niño/a para ver diferentes tipos de perros. Anime a su niño/a a que le pregunte al dueño de la tienda o a algún empleado acerca de las diferentes razas de los perros y sus necesidades.

How I Got a New Home

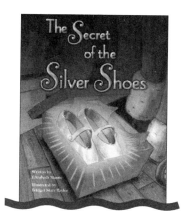

INTRODUCING THE PAIR-IT BOOKS

To introduce the topic of shoes, display the covers of *The Secret of the Silver Shoes* and *Shoes Through the Ages.* Encourage students to name different kinds of shoes they wear, such as dance shoes, snow boots, sneakers, and loafers. Record students' responses in a list on the left side of chart paper. Save the list for later.

The Secret of the Silver Shoes

A twin girl who doesn't feel very special finds a pair of magic silver shoes in her attic. When she puts the shoes on, she becomes invisible. However, when she begins to play tricks on her family and friends, she makes important discoveries about the shoes and life.

Key Vocabulary

ache	identical	shrink
budge	invisible	special
disappear	musty	stalk
hobble	mysteriously	throb

Objectives

Reading Strategy—Literary: Understanding author's purpose
Language Skill: Using contractions
Phonics/Word Study: Identifying *r*-controlled vowels *ar, or, er, ir, ur*
For more phonics practice, see *Steck-Vaughn Phonics* Level C, Unit 4, pages 93–94.

Additional Components

Audio Cassette: *The Secret of the Silver Shoes/Shoes Through the Ages*
Writing Masters, pages 105–108

Shoes Through the Ages

This nonfiction work explores the history of shoes, beginning with the Stone Age and continuing to the present. Unusual shoes such as crakows and chopines are described, as are shoes that originated many years ago and are still worn today.

Glossary Words

ancient	moccasin	sneaker
chopine	mule	sole
clog	patten	thong
crakow	slipper	upper

Other Key Vocabulary

bound	sabot
leather	trend
overshoe	

Objectives

Reading Strategy—Study Skills: Using text features
Language Skill: Using synonyms
Phonics/Word Study: Identifying multiple-meaning words
For more word study practice, see *Steck-Vaughn Phonics* Level C, Unit 7, pages 191–192.

Other Resources About Shoes

Father's Rubber Shoes, Yumi Heo
Shoes: Their History in Words and Pictures, Charlotte Yue and David Charlotte
Nasty Stinky Sneakers, Eve Bunting

The Secret of the Silver Shoes

BEFORE READING

Ask students to recall "Cinderella" and other stories that feature shoes. Discuss how the shoes are important in each story. Then have students scan the illustrations in *The Secret of the Silver Shoes* and predict what the secret is.

READING

To set a purpose for reading, ask students to read to find out what Piper learns in the story. Use questions such as these to guide the reading:

- *Why is Piper unhappy at the beginning of the story? (chapter 1)*
- *Why does Mrs. Carmelo think that her husband has a wild imagination? (chapter 4)*
- *What happens to the silver shoes each time Piper plays a trick on someone? (chapters 2–6)*
- *What should the silver shoes be used for? (chapter 6)*

AFTER READING

Have students discuss the predictions they made in Before Reading. Guide students to tell in their own words the lesson that Piper learns from wearing the silver shoes.

Writing Activities

Shoe Description
Materials: none

Invite a volunteer to read aloud the class list of shoes made in Introducing the Pair. Have each student choose a type of shoe and write a physical description of it. Allow time for students to share their description. Then discuss how the chosen shoes are similar and how they are different.

Silly Shoes
Materials: colored pencils or markers, unlined paper

Have students brainstorm a list of shoes that are used for special purposes, such as sports shoes, dancing shoes, and snow boots. Then ask students to think of a silly type of shoe that could be designed, such as a shoe to wear while doing math problems. Have students write a description of the shoe, including its special features. Then organize the class into pairs. Ask students to read their partner's description and draw the silly shoe.

MINI LESSONS

■ READING STRATEGY

Literacy: Understanding Author's Purpose

Explain that writers have different kinds of purposes for writing, such as to give information, to teach good behavior, and to entertain. Guide students to identify the author's purpose in *The Secret of the Silver Shoes (to teach good behavior)*. Help students name other books and stories that teach good behavior.

■ LANGUAGE SKILL

Using Contractions

Remind students that a contraction is a shortened form of two words and that the apostrophe takes the place of letters that are left out—for example, *I'm* is a shortening of *I* and *am*. Write on the board *"Let's play!" yelled Eva*. Ask volunteers to identify the contraction, to name the two words it stands for, and to identify the letter that was replaced by the apostrophe. Have students find other contractions in the book and write the two words from which each is made.

PHONICS/WORD STUDY

Identifying *r*-Controlled Vowels *ar, or, er, ir, ur*

Write *bar, fork, fern, bird,* and *burn* on the board and read each word aloud. Explain that when the letter *r* follows a vowel, it changes the sound of the vowel. Point out that the vowel in each word is neither short nor long and that *er, ir,* and *ur* all have the same sound. Then write *ar, or, er, ir,* and *ur* as headings on the board. Have students find words with these letter combinations in the book and write each word under the appropriate heading.

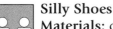

Shoes Through the Ages

BEFORE READING

Display *Shoes Through the Ages* and read the title aloud. Encourage students to examine the pictures in the book. Ask students which shoes look the most unusual, which look the most comfortable, and which look the most difficult to walk in.

READING

To set a purpose for reading, ask students to read to find out how shoes have changed since people first began to wear them. Use questions such as the following to guide the reading:

- *Why do people wear shoes? (chapter 1)*
- *What were the first shoes like? (chapter 2)*
- *What are some shoe fads from the past? (chapters 3–4)*
- *How did the king of England decide on shoe sizes? (chapter 5)*
- *How are modern shoes different from ancient ones? (chapters 2–5)*

AFTER READING

Invite students to write a type of shoe on a piece of paper, along with two or three pieces of information about it that can be used as clues. Have students give their clues one at a time so that classmates can guess the kind of shoe.

Writing Activities

A Day in the Life
Materials: none

Have students jot down what they did yesterday. Encourage them to add details about where they went, what the weather was like, and any special activities they may have done. Then have students write a journal entry or story about their day from their shoes' point of view.

Buy the Best!
Materials: newspapers, magazines

Provide magazines and newspapers and have students find shoe advertisements. Have them note the descriptive words used to sell the shoes and the way the ads are designed to attract readers. Then invite partners to create a magazine advertisement to encourage readers to buy a type of shoe.

MINI LESSONS

■ READING STRATEGY

Study Skills: Using Text Features

Explain to students that words next to a photograph or illustration that tell about it are called a caption. Tell students that reading a caption can help them better understand the photograph or illustration and that sometimes captions have very important information not contained in the body text. Have students turn to page 13 and read the caption. Ask a volunteer to tell what information the caption gives about the picture.

■ LANGUAGE SKILL

Using Synonyms

Write the synonyms *strong* and *powerful* on the board and explain that synonyms are words that have almost the same meaning. Point out that writers often use synonyms to avoid using the same word over and over and to make their writing more exact. Have partners look in Chapter 2 to find the synonym that the writer uses for each of the following words: *old*, *rich*, and *shone*. If students need help, suggest that they check a thesaurus or dictionary.

PHONICS/WORD STUDY

Identifying Multiple-Meaning Words

Explain to students that some words have more than one meaning. Write *bat* on the board and ask students to give two different meanings of the words. Help students look through the book to find multiple-meaning words such as *left*, *bark*, *leaves*, *points*, *bands*, *fine*, and *trip*. Write the words on the board. Then have partners write sentences that illustrate the meanings of each word.

Tying the Pair Together

Display the two books and ask students how the two are alike and different. Hve students identify the nonfiction book and the fiction one and explain how they know the difference between the two. Encourage students to share what they have learned about shoes from these two books.

Creative Art: Shoe Puzzlers
Materials: 8″ × 8″ posterboard squares, envelopes, markers, scissors

Invite students to draw a picture of a shoe from one of the books in the center of a square. Around their drawing, have them write several facts about the shoe, such as its uses, how it evolved, and its special features. Then have students cut their square into puzzle pieces, making sure that every piece has a word or part of the drawing. Students can place their pieces in an envelope and exchange puzzles.

Health: Taking Care of Our Feet
Materials: posterboard, markers

Invite students to suggest ways they can take good care of their feet. Students may suggest wearing shoes that fit, wearing socks to prevent blisters and keep the insides of shoes clean, choosing carefully when to walk barefoot, keeping toenails trimmed, always wearing shoes when moving heavy items or working with tools, and so on. Have students make a poster promoting foot health.

Math: Shoe Story Problems
Materials: none

Demonstrate how to make up a shoe story problem involving multiplying by two or counting by twos. An example follows:

The five Chang family members went for a walk. When they got home, they discovered that the baby had lost a shoe. How many shoes did the family come home with? (9)

Then have students create their own shoe story problems to share with the class.

Language Arts: Tongue-Twisting Performance
Materials: none

Read aloud the following tongue twister and invite students to say it back to you: *Silly Seth sat on Sally's silver sandals.* Ask students to take turns making up tongue twisters about different kinds of shoes. Challenge the rest of the class to repeat the twister.

ASSESSMENT

- Ask students to summarize their reading by retelling *The Secret of the Silver Shoes* and by telling about some kinds of shoes people have worn.
- Retell one of Aesop's fables and notice whether students can identify the moral in it.
- Display a picture and caption and ask students what the caption tells about the picture.
- Review samples of students' writings to assess comprehension of what they read.
- Use informal conferencing with students to assess comprehension and skill growth.

For further assessment see the checklist on pages 109–111.

Home Activities

Copy and distribute to students the *Take It Home* activity master on page 55 (English) or on page 56 (Spanish). Invite students to describe to their family the two main parts of their favorite shoes.

TAKE IT HOME

Dear Family of _____,

SHOE ACTIVITIES

Your child has been reading about shoes. *The Secret of the Silver Shoes* is a story about a girl who finds a pair of shoes that make her invisible. The shoes help her learn some valuable lessons. The companion book, *Shoes Through the Ages*, tells the history of shoes, from the animal-skin socks worn by Stone Age people to the many kinds of shoes worn today. To help your child learn more about shoes, choose from the activities below.

SHOE BOOKS

Help your child learn more about shoes by visiting the library. Check out *How Are Sneakers Made?* by Henry Horenstein, which tells how shoes are manufactured, and *Alligator Shoes* by Arthur Dorros, an engaging and easy-to-read Reading Rainbow book.

MOVIES AND MORE

Watch shoe movies such as *The Wizard of Oz* and *The Computer Wore Tennis Shoes* with your child. Talk about the special powers of Dorothy's red shoes. Ask your child who the shoe-wearing computer really is and discuss why the boy is called a computer.

You and your child may also want to make up a song about shoes.

ARTS AND CRAFTS: Fancy Soles

Materials: unlined paper, pencil, markers, glue, ribbon, shoe laces, other craft supplies (optional)

Choose one of your favorite shoes and ask your child to do the same. On separate sheets of paper, trace around each shoe sole. Use markers and other craft supplies to decorate the shoe outlines. Then make up stories about special powers that the shoes have. You may want to display your art for other family members to see.

SHARE

Visit a shoe store with your child and find as many different types of shoes as possible. Describe the color, materials, size, and other features of each kind of shoe. Talk about who might wear the type of shoe and when it might be worn.

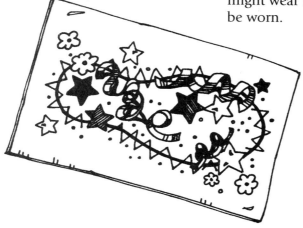

LLÉVAME A CASA

Estimada familia de _____,

ACTIVIDADES DE ZAPATOS

Su niño/a ha estado leyendo acerca de zapatos. *The Secret of the Silver Shoes* es un cuento acerca de una niña que encuentra un par de zapatos que la hacen invisible. Los zapatos le ayudan a aprender algunas lecciones valiosas. El libro compañero, *Shoes Through the Ages*, cuenta la historia de los zapatos, desde los calcetines de cuero de animales usados por la gente de la Edad de Piedra hasta los diferentes tipos de zapatos que se usan hoy. Para ayudarle a su niño/a a aprender más sobre zapatos, escoja de las actividades que siguen.

LIBROS DE ZAPATOS

Usted y su niño/a pueden aprender más sobre zapatos yendo a la biblioteca. Saquen *How Are Sneakers Made?* por Henry Horenstein, que cuenta cómo se fabrican los zapatos, y *Alligator Shoes* por Arthur Dorros, un libro de lectura de Rainbow, atractivo y fácil de leer.

PELÍCULAS Y MÁS

Vea películas tales como *The Wizard of Oz* y *The Computer Wore Tennis Shoes* con su niño/a. Conversen sobre los poderes especiales de los zapatos rojos de Dorothy. Pregúntele a su niño/a quién es realmente el computador que usa zapatos y conversen por qué llaman computador al niño.

ARTE Y ARTESANÍA: Suelas de fantasía

Materiales: papel sin líneas, lápiz, marcadores, goma de pegar, cinta, cordones de zapatos, otros materiales de artesanía (opcionales)

Escoja uno de sus zapatos favoritos y pídale a su niño/a que haga lo mismo. En hojas separadas de papel, tracen la suela de cada zapato. Usen marcadores y otros materiales para decorar el contorno del zapato. Luego inventen cuentos sobre poderes especiales que puedan tener los zapatos. Podrían exhibir su arte para que otros miembros de la familia lo vieran.

COMPARTAN

Visite una tienda de zapatos con su niño/a y busquen todos los tipos de zapatos diferentes que puedan encontrar. Describan el color, el material, el tamaño y otras características de cada zapato. Conversen acerca de quién podría usar ese tipo de zapatos y para qué ocasión.

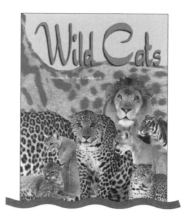

INTRODUCING THE PAIR-IT BOOKS

Display the two books and call on a student to read the titles aloud. Explain that one is a mystery about a wild cat that disappears from the zoo and that the other gives information about wild cats, including some lesser-known ones. Then have students name some kinds of wild cats and list them on the board. If students have difficulty, invite them to browse through the books.

The Mystery of the Missing Leopard

Clancy LaRue, feline detective, takes up the case of Midnight, a black leopard reportedly stolen from the city zoo. As the case unfolds, Clancy finds out that the leopard left on her own because she wants a zoo habitat, not a cage. The case ends happily with plans for raising money to build Midnight's habitat.

Key Vocabulary

bluff	habitat	pound
bristle	lunge	slink
dart	nocturnal	strut
feline	peer	suspicious

Objectives

Reading Strategy—Genre: Recognizing a mystery
Language Skill: Recognizing present tense
Phonics/Word Study: Identifying *y* as a vowel
For more phonics practice, see *Steck-Vaughn Phonics* Level C, Unit 4, pages 99–100.

Wild Cats

This nonfiction book presents a variety of wild cats, including the margay, caracal, serval, and other lesser-known ones.

Glossary Words

climate	keen	rosette
exhale	predator	scent
extinct	pride	species
flexible	reserve	stalk
habitat	retract	territory
home range		

Other Key Vocabulary

bound	graze
complex	prey
flutter	

Objectives

Reading Strategy—Literary: Distinguishing narration from exposition
Language Skill: Identifying comparatives and superlatives
Phonics/Word Study: Identifying syllables in VCCV and VCCCV words
For more word study practice, see *Steck-Vaughn Phonics* Level C, Unit 5, pages 137–138.

Additional Components

Audio Cassette: *The Mystery of the Missing Leopard/Wild Cats*
Writing Masters, pages 105–108

Other Resources About Wild Cats

Cats: In from the Wild, Caroline Arnold
The Wild Cat Crime (Nancy Drew Mystery), Carolyn M. Keene

The Mystery of the MISSING LEOPARD

BEFORE READING

Explain that *The Mystery of the Missing Leopard* is told by a house cat who is a detective. Then call on a few volunteers to read aloud book pages 3–5. Afterward ask students what they learned about the speaker and the tone of the story. Will the story be serious? Humorous? Sad?

READING

Encourage students to set a purpose for reading. Call on a few volunteers to share their purpose. Or suggest that students use the book title to set a purpose, asking themselves why the leopard is missing. Use questions such as these to guide the reading:

- *Can you describe Clancy LaRue's personality? (chapters 1–6)*
- *What steps does Clancy take to determine that Midnight was not stolen? (chapters 2–4)*
- *Why does Midnight end up at Jennifer's house? (chapters 5–6)*
- *How will people in the community help get Midnight a habitat? (chapter 6)*

AFTER READING

Call on volunteers to recall the things that Clancy does to locate Midnight. You may also want to have them compare Clancy to other detectives they know from books, television, and movies.

Writing Activities

Another Clancy LaRue Mystery
Materials: none

Invite students to write another Clancy LaRue mystery. Some may enjoy working in pairs to develop a story. They can divide the writing of the first draft and work together on a final draft.

Character Guessing Game
Materials: drawing paper, colored markers

Have small groups of students select a few familiar books of fiction, including *The Mystery of the Missing Leopard*. Ask students to review the books' main characters, write a paragraph in which a character introduces himself or herself, and draw a picture of the character. Invite students to present their introduction and the rest of the class to guess the character's name and the book title. As students present their introduction, they can hold the drawing so that the other students can't see it. When the correct answer is given, they can reveal the drawing.

■ READING STRATEGY

Genre: Recognizing a Mystery

Explain that mystery stories such as *The Mystery of the Missing Leopard* have several elements in common. Each one has a crime, a detective or two, and clues about who committed the crime. In the end the crime is solved. Ask students to identify each of these elements in the book.

■ LANGUAGE SKILL

Recognizing Present Tense

Remind students that stories have clues that tell readers when something is happening. Read aloud from the book, beginning with the third paragraph on page 3 and continuing to the end of page 4. Explain that verbs in the passage, such as *am* (in *I'm*), *is, smell, get up, stretch, finish,* and *do,* as well as the word *today,* let us know that Clancy is speaking in the present time. Call on volunteers to read aloud additional passages and to identify verbs and other clues that show the present tense.

PHONICS/WORD STUDY

Identifying *y* as a Vowel

Remind students that *y* is sometimes a vowel. Write these story words on the board: *mystery, my, family, myself, easy, sunny, try, shiny,* and *by.* Underline each *y.* Read several words aloud and identify the sound of the *y;* call on volunteers to do the same for the remaining words. Point out that when a word with one syllable ends in *y,* the *y* usually has a long *i* sound. When the *y* is in the middle of a syllable, it usually has the short *i* sound. When a word with two or more syllables ends in *y,* the *y* usually has the long *e* sound.

Wild Cats

BEFORE READING

Write these words on the chalkboard: *lion, leopard, tiger, cheetah.* Then activate students' prior knowledge by talking about wild cats. If necessary, prompt students to think about wild cats' food, appearance, behavior, and natural habitats.

READING

Invite students to set a purpose for reading. If necessary, ask students to read to learn new information about wild cats they are familiar with and to learn the names of wild cats unfamiliar to them. Use questions such as these to guide the reading:

- *How are wild cats alike? (chapter 1)*
- *Which big cats live and hunt in groups? Which big cats live alone? (chapters 2–5)*
- *How is a cheetah different from other wild cats? (chapter 6)*
- *What does a serval look like? (chapter 7)*
- *Which human activities have endangered wild cats? (chapter 8)*

AFTER READING

Ask students to tell which facts and wild cats they find most interesting. Have them give page references in case other students want to locate them.

Writing Activities

Wild Cats Then and Now
Materials: information books about wild cats

Talk with students about why some wild cats have become endangered. Then have students write a report on a wild cat for which you have reference materials. Students should include any changes in the population of their wild cat. If possible, they should also write whether the wild cat has a smaller or larger range now than in the past. If the range has changed, have students explain why. Bind the reports into a class book entitled *Wild Cats Then and Now.*

In Search of the Wild Cat
Materials: information books about wild cats

Tell students that some tourists travel to places where they can see wild animals in their natural habitat. Have small groups of students prepare and present a wild cat tour for classmates. Groups should select a wild cat and conduct research so that they can write what a tour guide would say about the wild cat, including its habitat, the number left in the wild, its habits, and the activities tourists may be able to observe.

> ## MINI LESSONS

■ READING STRATEGY

Literary: Distinguishing Narration from Exposition

Explain that there are two types of writing in *Wild Cats.* One type tells a story. The other type gives facts. Have students read pages 11 and 12. Guide students to understand that page 11 (narration) tells a story and page 12 (exposition) gives facts. Then have students browse through chapters 4 and 5 and identify story text and fact text.

■ LANGUAGE SKILL

Identifying Comparatives and Superlatives

Write *Jaguars are <u>shorter</u> and <u>stockier</u> than their leopard cousins* and *Tigers are the <u>largest</u> members of the cat family* on the board. Have a student read the sentences aloud. Explain that the underlined words describe by making a comparison. Then have students look for other comparatives and superlatives in the book.

PHONICS/WORD STUDY

Identifying Syllables in VCCV and VCCCV Words

Write *roar, mountain, breathe, purr, attack,* and *bottom* on the board and ask students to identify the words with two syllables. Point out the VCCV pattern in *mountain, attack,* and *bottom* and draw lines between the syllables. Next write *instance, complex, hungry,* and *surprise* and point out the VCCCV pattern. Again, draw lines to show the syllables. Explain that these words are usually divided between the first two consonants.

Tying the Pair Together

Print the names of several wild cats on cards and fold them so that the names can't be seen. Organize the class into small groups and have a group representative select a card. Then ask the group to design a zoo habitat for the wild cat. Invite groups to present their habitat to the rest of the class.

Science: Good Zoos
Materials: information books about wild cats

Encourage students to learn about good zoo areas for wild cats and to report their findings. Two good books on the topic are *Keepers of the Kingdom* by Michael Nichols, and *Zoo Book* by Linda Koebner.

Mathematics: Comparing Wild Cats
Materials: encyclopedias, information books about wild cats

Have students find numeric facts about wild cats, such as average length, weight, life span, number of babies, and amount of food eaten weekly or daily. Then have students use these facts to write story problems for a partner to solve. For example, a student might write *A lion weighs 500 pounds. A mountain lion weighs 200 pounds. How much heavier is the lion?*

Writing: Wild Cat Poetry
Materials: none

Write the following poem on the board:

Loud,
Lazy,
Lives in prides,
Loves meat,
Lion!

Point out that each line in this poem begins with *L*, the first letter in *lion* and that the facts come from the book *Wild Cats*. Ask students to write similar poems about other wild cats.

Art: What Kind of Coat?
Materials: watercolor paints, 6″ × 6″ pieces of drawing paper, poster board, razor knife

Invite students to make a display of wild cats' distinctive colors and patterns. Help students cut six 5″ × 5″ flaps in a piece of posterboard. Then have students paint swatches of the fur of six wild cats. Students can tape the swatches behind the flaps so the "fur" can be seen when the flaps are opened. Students can print the cat's name and habitat on the flap.

ASSESSMENT

- Ask students to retell *The Mystery of the Missing Leopard* and to describe one or two of the wild cats in *Wild Cats.*
- Have students explain how they know a story is a mystery.
- Read aloud a fiction and a nonfiction passage. Ask students which tells a story and which provides information.
- Review samples of students' writing to assess comprehension of what they read.
- Use informal conferencing with students to assess comprehension and skill growth.

For further assessment, see the checklist on pages 109–111.

Home Activities

Copy and distribute to children the *Take It Home* activity master on page 61 (English) or page 62 (Spanish). Invite students to discuss with their family what they learned about wild cats.

Dear Family of _____,

WILD CAT ACTIVITIES

Your child has been reading about wild cats. *The Mystery of the Missing Leopard* features a black leopard that disappears from a zoo, along with a clever cat detective. *Wild Cats*, a nonfiction book, describes several different species of wild cats. To help your child learn more about wild cats, choose from the activities below.

WILD CAT BOOKS

Help your child learn more about wild cats by visiting the local library and looking for books such as *Cats: In from the Wild* by Caroline Arnold, *A Lion Named Shirley* by Bernard Waber, and *Clue at the Zoo* by Patricia Giff Reilly.

MOVIES AND MORE

View movies and videos about wild cats. National Geographic's *Really Wild Animals: Totally Tropical* shows wild cats and other animals in their natural habitat. *Tiger!* from the National Wildlife Federation is about tigers in India. *Eyewitness: Cat* shows the similarities between wild cats and house cats.

ARTS AND CRAFTS: Wild Clay Cats
Materials: clay (various colors), toothpicks, uncooked spaghetti, unlined paper, markers

With your child make one or two wild cats out of clay, using toothpicks to add features such as stripes and spots. Break the spaghetti into very small pieces and use it for whiskers. Draw a picture of the place where each wild cat lives and display the drawing with the clay figure.

SHARE

Our language includes many words for the things that cats do and for the ways they move—for example, *stalk, pounce, slink, leap, claw, dart,* and *stretch.* Together think of more words. Then take turns acting out words for each other to guess.

LLÉVAME A CASA

Estimada familia de _____,

ACTIVIDADES DE GATOS MONTESES

Su niño/a ha estado leyendo acerca de gatos monteses. *The Mystery of the Missing Leopard* presenta un leopardo negro que desaparece del zoológico, con un gato detective muy listo. *Wild Cats*, un libro de no-ficcion, describe varias especies de gatos monteses. Para ayudarle a su niño/a a aprender más sobre gatos monteses, escoja de las actividades que siguen.

LIBROS DE GATOS MONTESES

Ayúdele a su niño/a a aprender más sobre gatos monteses yendo a la biblioteca y buscando libros tales como *Cats: In from the Wild* por Caroline Arnold, *A Lion Named Shirley* por Bernard Waber y *Clue at the Zoo* por Patricia Giff Reilly.

PELÍCULAS Y MÁS

Vean películas y videos de gatos monteses. *Really Wild Animals: Totally Tropical* de la National Geographic muestra gatos monteses y otros animales en su hábitat natural. *Tiger!* de la National Wildlife Federation trata de tigres en la India. *Eyewitness: Cat* muestra las semejanzas entre gatos monteses y gatos domésticos.

ARTE Y ARTESANÍA: Gatos monteses hechos de arcilla

Materiales: arcilla (de varios colores), mondadientes, espaguetis crudos, papel sin líneas, marcadores

Haga uno o dos gatos monteses de arcilla con su niño/a usando los mondadientes para agregar detalles tales como rayas o manchas. Quiebren los espaguetis en pedacitos y úselos para bigotes. Hagan un dibujo del lugar donde vive cada gato montés y expongan el dibujo con la figura de arcilla.

COMPARTAN

Nuestro idioma incluye muchas palabras para describir las cosas que hacen los gatos y la forma como se mueven — por ejemplo, *caminar sigilosamente*, *abalanzarse*, *escabullirse*, *saltar*, *arañar*, *precipitars* y *estirarse*. Piensen en otras palabras. Luego tomen turnos para actuar las palabras para que el otro las adivine.

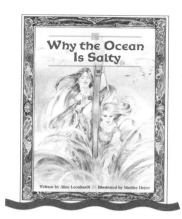

INTRODUCING THE PAIR-IT BOOKS

To introduce the topic of oceans, display the covers of *Why the Ocean Is Salty* and *Ocean Life: Tide Pool Creatures*. Call on a student to read the titles aloud. Ask another student to identify the word that is in both titles. Make a word web on chart paper, writing *ocean* in the center. Invite students to share ideas about oceans. Record their responses on the web.

Why the Ocean Is Salty

The god of the ocean sends his daughters to help the king of Iceland. Locked in the grip of a long winter, the king's country is starving. The ocean god's daughters use magic millstones to bring spring—and food. The king and others, however, become greedy. The maidens' last gift is a surprise.

Key Vocabulary

bow (ship)	greed	millstones
coast	idle	minerals
conquer	longship	pourquoi
driftwood	maiden	tide

Objectives

Reading Strategy—Genre: Recognizing a pourquoi tale
Language Skill: Identifying adjectives
Phonics/Word Study: Understanding words from other languages

Ocean Life: Tide Pool Creatures

The text, photographs, and diagrams of this book introduce students to the ecology of tide pools, with a special emphasis on the rich variety of animal life in this habitat.

Glossary Words

adapt	high tide	predator
algae	inhabitant	proboscis
bivalve	larvae	scavenger
camouflage	low tide	tentacle
crevice	pincer	

Other Key Vocabulary

barnacle	sea urchin
limpet	tide pool
sea anemone	

Objectives

Reading Strategy—Study Skills: Interpreting diagrams
Language Skill: Identifying linking verbs
Phonics/Word Study: Identifying compound words
For more word study practice, see *Steck-Vaughn Phonics* Level C, Unit 5, pages 125–126.

Additional Components

Audio Cassette: *Why the Ocean Is Salty/ Ocean Life: Tide Pool Creatures*
Writing Masters, pages 105–108

Other Resources About Oceans

What About Oceans?, Steck-Vaughn
Animals of the Oceans, Stephen Savage
When the Tide Is Low, Sheila Cole
Exploring Water Habitats CD-ROM, Steck-Vaughn

Why the Ocean Is Salty

BEFORE READING

Ask students who have visited an ocean to share their ocean experiences. Have them describe the water in the ocean (salty) and ask them to suggest some reasons why the ocean is salty. Write their ideas on the board.

READING

To set a purpose for reading, ask students to read to find out how the maidens on the cover helped the people of Iceland. Use questions such as these to guide the reading:

- *Why is King Ari troubled? (chapter 1)*
- *What things does King Ari want the maidens to do? (chapters 2 and 3)*
- *What things make the maidens unhappy? (chapter 3)*
- *How does greed spoil the happiness of the island people? (chapter 4)*

AFTER READING

Have students compare and contrast the reasons they gave for the ocean's saltiness in Before Reading with the scientific explanation in the introduction and with the explanation in the tale itself.

Writing Activities

Creating a Pourquoi Tale
Materials: audio cassette recorder and audio cassette

Invite groups of students to write their own pourquoi tale. Possible titles include *Why Does the Dog Wag Its Tail?* and *How Did the Skunk Get Its Smell?* Allow groups to read aloud or act out their story for classmates. Some groups may wish to record their story on audio cassette to share with others.

Ocean Song
Materials: chart paper, marker

Lead students in singing "I've Been Working on the Railroad." Then invite students to write new words for the tune that retell all or part of *Why the Ocean Is Salty*. For example, students might begin with the following lines:

We've been waiting for the springtime,
All the live-long day.
We've been waiting for the springtime,
Just to grow some wheat and hay.

MINI LESSONS

■ READING STRATEGY

Genre: Recognizing a Pourquoi Tale

Direct students' attention to the word *Why* in the title of the book. Ask students why the ocean is salty, according to the tale. Explain that many pourquoi tales were made up long ago by people who were trying to explain something in nature. Point out that many of the titles start with *Why* or *How*. Share other pourquoi tales, such as *How the Stars Fell into the Sky*, *How the Guinea Fowl Got Her Spots*, and *Why Mosquitoes Buzz in People's Ears*.

■ LANGUAGE SKILL

Identifying Adjectives

Tell students that an adjective is a word that describes by telling which one, what kind of, how many, or how much. Have students reread the first two sentences on page 4 and identify the adjectives in the sentences. List the adjectives on the board and discuss the question that each one answers.

PHONICS/WORD STUDY

Understanding Words from Other Languages

Reread the introduction on page 3 with students, pointing out that the word *pourquoi* is borrowed from the French language and that it means *why*. Tell students that other French words and phrases, including *café* ("restaurant"), *au gratin* ("with cheese"), and *bon voyage* ("have a good trip") are often used in English. Explain to students the meaning of each.

Ocean Life: Tide Pool Creatures

BEFORE READING

Talk with students about what a tide pool is—a pool of seawater left behind when the ocean is pulled away from the shore. Display the cover of the book and point out the starfish and sea anemones. Tell students this book has facts about these and other interesting animals found in tide pools.

READING

To set a purpose for reading, ask students to read to learn more about the animals that live in tide pools. Use questions such as these to guide the reading:

- *What is the difference between high tide and low tide? (chapter 1)*
- *In what ways do tide pool animals protect themselves? (chapters 2–9)*
- *What do tide pool animals eat? (chapters 2–9)*
- *What makes life in a tide pool tricky? (chapters 1 and 10)*

AFTER READING

On the board write the names of tide pool animals. Have each student choose an animal and say one thing he or she learned about the animal by reading the book.

Writing Activities

Ocean Poetry
Materials: writing or drawing paper, crayons

Invite partners to write a three-line poem about a tide pool creature. Write the following directions and example on the board. Invite partners to illustrate and display their poem.

1. *Write the name of the animal.*
2. *Write three words that tell more about it.*
3. *Write a nickname for the animal.*

Sea scorpion
Fierce spiny fish
Spike

Sea Shapes
Materials: construction paper, markers

Invite students to choose an animal from the book, draw its shape on construction paper, and cut out the shape. Have them write facts about the animal on the shape, such as the animal's name and features and what it eats. If possible, provide encyclopedias and nature magazines so students can include additional information on their shape. Display the shapes on a tide pool bulletin board.

MINI LESSONS

■ READING STRATEGY

Study Skills: Interpreting Diagrams

Tell students that a diagram is a picture that shows the parts of something or the order in which something happens. Direct students' attention to the diagram of the crab on page 18. Encourage students to read the diagram in this manner:

1. *Look at the diagram to decide what it shows. If the diagram has a title, read it to help you decide.*
2. *Look at any parts of the diagram.*
3. *Read the labels.*
4. *Think about how all the pieces fit together.*

Then have students look at the diagram of the dog whelk life cycle on page 34 and follow the same steps.

■ LANGUAGE SKILL

Identifying Linking Verbs

Write on the board *A shanny is a fish.* Help students identify the two words that are linked by the verb *is* (*shanny, fish*). Remind students that a linking verb does not show action. It links, or connects, the subject of a sentence to a word in the predicate. Ask students to look in the book to find some linking verbs and the words they link. For example, in the first paragraph on page 3, the linking verb *is* appears three times.

PHONICS/WORD STUDY

Identifying Compound Words

Write the word *seashell* on the board. Ask a student to identify the two words that make up this compound word (*sea, shell*). Then ask students to brainstorm compound words that have the word *sea* or *fish* in them (*seawater, seabird, seaweed, starfish, jellyfish, pipefish, clingfish*).

Tying the Pair Together

Display the two books and ask students to compare and contrast them. Ask students to share other information they know about oceans, including information about the plants and animals that live in the ocean, people who live near oceans and the kind of work they do, and ships that travel on the oceans.

Science: Creature Features
Materials: 3 index cards per group

Give each group three index cards and ask students to write one characteristic of a tide pool creature on each card. Groups should exchange cards and write on the reverse side of each the names of the creatures with that characteristic. Discuss students' responses with them and have them make revisions as needed.

Social Studies: Oceans of the World
Materials: globe or physical world map

Display a globe or world map and guide students in exploring the locations of the oceans and seas. Then invite groups to play What's My Name? Begin by giving the clue *I am a sea between New Guinea and Australia* and demonstrating how to locate the Coral Sea. Have groups continue the game on their own. Group members should take turns giving clues.

Language Arts: A Class Yarn
Materials: 40 pieces of yarn, each about 10" long

Wind the yarn into a ball, one piece at a time. Tell students that they are going to make up a class yarn, or story, about the ocean and that each student will have a turn to tell a part of the story. Demonstrate how to unwind one piece of yarn as you begin the story with a few sentences such as *One day Pat decided to take his dog King for a walk near the ocean. He wondered what treasures he might find.* When you reach the end of the first piece of yarn, hand the ball to a student, who should continue the story.

Creative Arts: Tide Pool Habitat
Materials: mural paper, crayons, aprons, diluted blue watercolor paint, large paintbrushes

Divide a long sheet of mural paper in half vertically and add the labels *High Tide* and *Low Tide*. Have students draw tide pools on each half. Then have students paint the *High Tide* half with diluted blue watercolor. The crayons should resist the paint and give that part of the mural an underwater effect.

ASSESSMENT

- Ask students to summarize their reading by naming and describing some animals that live in tide pools and by retelling the explanation for the ocean's salty water in *Why the Ocean Is Salty*.
- Observe whether students can recognize a pourquoi tale in literature that you share with them.
- Display a simple labeled diagram and ask students to tell about it. You might draw the underside of a starfish and label the mouth, arms, eyespots, and tube feet.
- Review samples of students' writings to assess comprehension of what they read.
- Use informal conferencing with students to assess comprehension and skill growth.

For further assessment see the checklist on pages 109–111.

Home Activities

Copy and distribute to students the Take It Home activity master on page 67 (English) or on page 68 (Spanish). Invite students to retell the story *Why the Ocean Is Salty* to family members.

TAKE IT HOME

Dear Family of _____,

OCEAN ACTIVITIES

Your child has been reading about oceans. *Why the Ocean Is Salty* is an Icelandic tale about a king who seeks help when his people are starving. The companion book, *Ocean Life: Tide Pool Creatures*, describes animals that live at the edge of the ocean. To help your child learn more about oceans, use the activities below.

OCEAN BOOKS

Help your child learn more about oceans by visiting the library. Check out *The Magic School Bus on the Ocean Floor* by Joanna Cole and Bruce Degan and *I Wonder Why the Sea Is Salty: and Other Questions About the Oceans* by Anita Ganeri and Tony Kenyon.

MOVIES AND MORE

View movies such as *The Little Mermaid* and *Zeus and Roxanne* with your child. Talk about how life in and around an ocean is presented in each.

You may want to play recordings of sounds from the ocean, such as ocean waves and whale sounds.

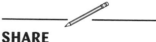

ARTS AND CRAFTS: Undersea Picture

Materials: white construction paper, clear glue, watercolor paints, paintbrush

Have your child draw some seashells on white construction paper. Help your child use clear glue to trace and fill in the shells. When the glue dries completely, your child can paint over the shells with watercolors to make an undersea picture. Allow the picture to dry overnight.

SHARE

If possible, visit a city aquarium or local pet shop with your child to look at ocean fish and other sea creatures. Encourage your child to ask the guide or shopkeeper questions about the animals and their habitat. Then ask your child to write about the trip.

LLÉVAME A CASA

Estimada familia de _____,

ACTIVIDADES DE MAR

Su niño/a ha estado leyendo acerca del mar. *Why the Ocean Is Salty* es un cuento islandés sobre un rey que pide ayuda cuando su pueblo está pasando hambre. El libro compañero, *Ocean Life: Tide Pool Creatures*, describe animales que viven al borde del mar. Para ayudarle a su niño/a a aprender más acerca del mar, utilice las actividades que siguen.

LIBROS DE MAR

Visite la biblioteca con su niño/a para ayudarle a aprender más sobre el mar. Saquen *The Magic School Bus on the Ocean Floor* por Joanna Cole y Bruce Degan o *I Wonder Why the Sea Is Salty: and Other Questions About the Oceans* por Anita Ganeri y Tony Kenyon.

PELÍCULAS Y MÁS

Vea películas tales como *The Little Mermaid* y *Zeus and Roxanne* con su niño/a. Conversen acerca de cómo se presenta la vida en el mar y a su alrededor en cada película.

Pueden tocar grabaciones de sonidos del mar, tales como el ruido de las olas y los sonidos de las ballenas.

ARTE Y ARTESANÍA: DIBUJO SUBMARINO

Materiales: papel blanco de construcción, goma de pegar, acuarela, pincel

Pídale a su niño/a que dibuje conchas de mar en el papel blanco de construcción. Ayúdele a usar la goma de pegar transparente para trazar el contorno de las conchas y rellenarlas. Cuando la goma se haya secado completamente, su niño/a puede pintar sobre las conchas con acuarelas para hacer un cuadro submarino. Permitan que el cuadro se seque durante la noche.

COMPARTAN

Si fuera posible, visiten un acuario o una tienda local de mascotas para mirar peces de mar y otras criaturas marinas. Anime a su niño/a a que haga preguntas al guía o al dueño de la tienda sobre los animales y sus hábitats. Luego pídale a su niño/a que escriba acerca del paseo.

INTRODUCING THE PAIR-IT BOOKS

Have volunteers read aloud the titles of the two books. Explain that *Diary of a Pioneer Boy* is fiction and *The Pioneer Way* is nonfiction. To preview the places included in the books, display a map of North America and have volunteers point out the East Coast, the Appalachian and Rocky mountains, the Mississippi River, the Great Plains and the states of Missouri, Montana, Arizona, New Mexico, and California.

Diary of a Pioneer Boy

In the spring of 1885, young Ben Wilkins and his family leave St. Louis for Montana, where they hope to become successful cattle ranchers. Ben is eager for grown-up responsibilities—and adventure! That's just what he gets when he becomes lost in fog not far from the family's new Montana homestead.

Key Vocabulary

boulder	jerky	rickety
envy	mission	sagebrush
gully	notch	trolley
hitch	reed	

Objectives

Reading Strategy—Genre: Recognizing historical fiction

Language Skill: Distinguishing between points of view

Phonics/Word Study: Recognizing suffixes *-ness, -y, -ful, -ly*

For more word study practice, see *Steck-Vaughn Phonics* Level C, Unit 6, pages 167–168.

Additional Components

Audio Cassette: *Diary of a Pioneer Boy/ The Pioneer Way*

Writing Masters, pages 105–108

The Pioneer Way

This book is an overview of the Westward Movement in North America. Students learn about how pioneers traveled, where they settled, and how they used varied natural resources to build homes.

Glossary Words

adobe	flatboat	prairie schooner
chink	frontier	reservation
Conestoga wagon	general store	sod
	lean-to	wagon train
dugout	merchant	wilderness

Other Key Vocabulary

arch	hardship
axle	supplies

Objectives

Reading Strategy—Study Skills: Using parts of a book

Language Skill: Understanding pronouns and antecedents

Phonics/Word Study: Understanding sounds of *air, are, ear, eer*

For more phonics practice, see *Steck-Vaughn Phonics* Level C, Unit 4, pages 95–96.

Other Resources About Pioneers

Go West! The Homesteaders Challenge CD-ROM, Steck-Vaughn

Sacagawea, Steck-Vaughn

Diary of a Pioneer Boy

BEFORE READING

Have students page through the book, identify the diary entries, and examine the illustrations. Then call on volunteers to read aloud the first paragraph of the first diary entry.

READING

To set a purpose for reading, suggest that students read to find out what hardships and dangers Ben and his family face in the story. Use questions such as the following to guide the reading:

- *How is Ben different from Conrad and Sarah? (chapter 1)*
- *How does Ben end up alone and lost? (chapter 2)*
- *What things happen to Ben when he is with Mary Fields? (chapters 3–7)*
- *What nice thing does Ben do for Suzanne? What nice thing does Suzanne do for Ben? (chapter 6)*

AFTER READING

Have students page through the book again and compare the diary entries and the other narrative text in the story. Discuss how the two kinds of text are different and which kind students prefer.

Writing Activities

Book Review
Materials: colored pencils

Invite students to write a review of the book in the form of a diary entry. Have them begin with *Dear Diary, Today I finished a book about…*. Encourage them to write what they like and don't like about the story. Have students read or explain their entries to a partner.

Timeline
Materials: butcher paper, large index cards, colored pencils or markers, push pins or tape

Have small groups of students plan and create an illustrated timeline of the story. Groups should first review the book and decide on several important dates and events. Then the group should draw a horizontal bar on the butcher paper, making tick marks and adding the dates of events. Each student can write a summary of a few events on index cards, which can be attached above or below the appropriate points on the time line.

■ READING STRATEGY

Genre: Recognizing Historical Fiction

Explain that stories that include realistic characters and events from the past are called *historical fiction*. To reinforce the definition, discuss the time period and events of *Diary of a Pioneer Boy*. Then discuss other selected fiction books and ask students whether they are historical or contemporary fiction.

■ LANGUAGE SKILL

Distinguishing Between Points of View

Remind students that the book has two kinds of text: Ben's diary entries and the paragraphs in between. Read aloud pages 5 and 6. Explain that page 5 is written by someone who is not a part of the story and that page 6 is written by Ben, who is part of the story. Guide students to see that the pronouns provide clues about who is telling the story.

PHONICS/WORD STUDY

Recognizing Suffixes *-ness, -y, -ful, -ly*

Remind students that words are often made up of parts. Explain that a suffix is a word part added to the end of a base word to change its meaning. Write *darkness, sharpness, misty, bumpy, careful, hopeful, wildly,* and *slowly* on the board and underline the suffixes. Invite students to explain what the suffixes mean. As needed, explain that *-ness* and *-y* mean "having" or "the state of being"; *-ful* means "with" or "full of"; and *-ly* means "in that way."

The Pioneer Way

BEFORE READING

Call on volunteers to explain why families of today move from one home to another. Discuss with students how family members decide which possessions to take with them and which to leave behind.

READING

Help students set a purpose for reading. Ask them to think about how the moves of modern families are different from the pioneers' as they read. Use questions such as these to guide the reading:

- *What are some of the reasons why people decided to move west? (Introduction and chapter 1)*
- *What kinds of problems did the pioneers face on the way west? (chapters 2 and 3)*
- *What useful things did pioneers find in the places they moved to? How did they use these things? (chapters 4, 5)*
- *How did pioneer families help each other? (chapters 6, 7)*

AFTER READING

Call on volunteers to tell some differences between the moves of modern families and pioneer families. To record students' thoughts, make a Venn diagram with the labels *Modern Family Moves, Both,* and *Pioneer Moves.*

Writing Activities

Many Uses for Many Things
Materials: encyclopedias, information books about pioneers

Pioneers often had more than one use for resources. Write *ax, oxen, Conestoga wagon, seeds, plow, logs, water, rocks, corn, mud, sod, reeds, adobe,* and *animal skins* on the board. Have small groups of students choose 5 items from this list and brainstorm and research different ways in which each item could be used. Ask students to write their ideas for each item on an index card. The class can then put their cards in alphabetical order and staple them to make a small reference book.

To Go or Not to Go
Materials: none

Ask students to imagine that they are adults living in an East Coast city in the 1870s. Each student is the parent of three children and must make the decision whether to leave home and settle in the West. Generate with the class a list of the pros and cons for moving to the West. Then have each student write a paragraph explaining his or her decision.

■ READING STRATEGY

Study Skills: Using Parts of a Book

Have students refer to the table of contents, glossary, and index of the book as you explain the uses of each. Give students practice in using the parts of a book by asking them questions such as *What part of this book should I look in to find out what the word* sod *means?*

■ LANGUAGE SKILL

Understanding Pronouns and Antecedents

Explain that pronouns replace nouns in writing so we don't have to repeat the nouns. Write the pronouns *they, them,* and *their* on the board and ask students to listen for them as you read page 20 aloud. Then write *The curve kept things inside the wagon from sliding out when it went up and down over hills* on the board and underline *it.* Ask students what *it* refers to. You may wish to have students locate more pronouns in the book and identify the antecedent for each.

PHONICS/WORD STUDY

Understanding Sounds of *air, are, ear, eer*

List the following words on the board in four columns, according to spelling pattern: *chair, prairie; care, share; bear, pear, heard, learn, year, clear;* and *pioneer, deer.* Point out the spelling patterns and have students read the lists aloud. Then invite volunteers to use colored chalk in three different colors to underline the *r*-controlled patterns that are sounded alike (*chair, prairie, care, share, bear, pear; year, clear, pioneer, deer; heard, learn*).

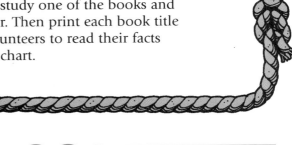

Tying the Pair Together

Give each student several minutes to study one of the books and write a few facts, one per slip of paper. Then print each book title on a piece of chart paper. Call on volunteers to read their facts aloud and attach them to the correct chart.

Geography: Mapping the Routes West
Materials: encyclopedias, information books about the Westward Movement, drawing paper, colored pencils

Divide the class into small groups and encourage them to research the major trails to the West (Oregon Trail, Santa Fe Trail, and Chisholm Trail). Have students draw a map of the United States and mark on it the trails, rivers, and mountains. Encourage students to include additional information, such as the dates the trails were used, the number of people who used them, and the difficulties travelers encountered.

Mathematics: Planning a Sod House
Materials: pictures of sod houses, sheets of lightweight cardboard, rulers, tape, scissors

Have students examine pictures of sod houses and then experiment to find out about how many sod bricks would be needed to make a house 12 feet by 20 feet. Encourage students to begin by making a cardboard model. Explain that students should consider the size of the sod bricks and the height of the walls.

Art: Patchwork Quilt
Materials: books of traditional quilt designs, rulers, fabric scraps, needles, thread, scissors

Have students study pioneer quilts. Each student can then design and make a quilt square. Squares can be sewn directly to each other or to long divider strips. Hang the finished quilt on a classroom wall.

Language Arts: Pioneer Supplies
Materials: none

Have students imagine that they are 19th-century pioneers moving to the West or future pioneers moving to a planet in our solar system. Students should list the things they would bring with them on the journey and the reasons for bringing each. Tell students to think about what they would need to survive and whether they could find these things on their journey. Allow students time to discuss their list.

ASSESSMENT

- Present students with unfamiliar fiction and nonfiction books. Have students identify the historical fiction book.
- Ask students what information a nonfiction book's table of contents, glossary, and index give.
- Present students with passages containing pronouns and ask them to identify the pronouns or antecedents or both.
- Review samples of students' writing to assess comprehension of what they read.
- Use informal conferencing with students to assess comprehension and skill growth.

For further assessment see the checklist on pages 109–111.

Home Activities

Copy and distribute to students the *Take It Home* activity master on page 73 (English) or page 74 (Spanish). Invite students to discuss pioneer life with their family.

Dear Family of _____,

PIONEER ACTIVITIES

Your child has been reading about settlers of the North American frontier. A fiction book called *Diary of a Pioneer Boy* tells the story of a boy whose family moves from Missouri to Montana in 1885. *The Pioneer Way* is an nonfiction book that describes many aspects of pioneer life: how pioneers traveled and where they settled, farming methods, food sources, children's education, and home construction.

PIONEER BOOKS

You and your child can find more books about pioneers by visiting the library. Check out the nonfiction book *Children of the Westward Trail* by Rebecca Stefoff. For an interesting story written as a journal and illustrated with photographs taken at "living history" sites, check out *Joshua's Westward Journal* by Joan Anderson.

MOVIES AND MORE

View pioneer movies such as the classic *Westward Ho* with your child. Discuss with your child the dangers that the pioneers face in the film.

ARTS AND CRAFTS: Journey Cakes
Materials: 2 eggs, 1 cup water, 3/4 cup milk, 2 tbsp. oil, 1 tsp. salt, 2 cups cornmeal

The pioneers ate a lot of corn! Mix the first five ingredients. Then stir in the cornmeal until the batter is smooth. Fry 1/4 cup of batter for each cake. Serve with butter and syrup.

SHARE

Keep a diary of a trip or vacation that you take with your child. To make a diary, buy an inexpensive notebook and cover it with special paper. Each day, write an entry on the left pages, and have your child write and draw pictures on the right pages. Take along a glue stick and scissors, too, so you can add postcards, tickets, and other mementos.

Estimada familia de _____,

ACTIVIDADES DE PIONEROS

Su niño/a ha estado leyendo sobre colonos de la frontera norteamericana. Un libro de ficción llamado *Diary of a Pioneer Boy* cuenta la historia de un niño cuya familia se muda de Missouri a Montana en 1885. *The Pioneer Way* es un libro de no ficción que describe varios aspectos de la vida de los colonos: cómo viajaban y dónde se instalaban, métodos de cultivos, fuentes de alimentos, educación de los niños y construcción de casas.

LIBROS DE PIONEROS

Usted y su niño/a pueden encontrar más libros sobre pioneros si visitan la biblioteca. Saquen prestado el libro de no ficción, *Children of the Westward Trail* por Rebecca Stefoff. Para leer una historia interesante escrita como un diario e ilustrada con fotografías tomadas en "lugares de historia viva", saquen *Joshua's Westward Journal* por Joan Anderson.

ARTE Y ARTESANÍA: Pasteles para el viaje

Materiales: 2 huevos, 1 taza de agua, de taza de leche, 2 cucharadas de aceite, 1 cucharadita de sal, 2 tazas de harina de maíz (cornmeal)

¡Los pioneros comían mucho maíz! Mezclen los cinco primeros ingredientes. Luego mezclen la harina maiz hasta que la mezcla esté suave. Frían de taza de la mezcla para cada pastel. Sírvanlos con mantequilla y almíbar.

PELÍCULAS Y MÁS

Vea películas de pioneros tales como *Westward Ho* con su niño/a. Conversen sobre los peligros que enfrentan los pioneros en la película.

COMPARTAN

Escriba un diario cuando salga de paseo o de vacaciones con su niño/a. Para hacer un diario, compren un cuaderno barato y fórrenlo con un papel especial. Cada día, escriban una anotación en las páginas del lado izquierdo y dibujen en las páginas del lado derecho. Lleven una barra adhesiva y también unas tijeras para que puedan agregar tarjetas postales, boletos y otros recuerdos.

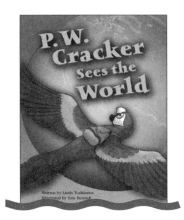

INTRODUCING THE PAIR-IT BOOKS

To introduce the topic of geography, display the covers of *P.W. Cracker Sees the World* and *Our World of Wonders*. Have students read the titles and compare the covers. Ask which word is the same in both titles. Then make a two-column chart on the board. Ask students to name countries they would like to visit and why. Record the countries and reasons in the columns on the board.

P.W. Cracker Sees the World

The class parrot, P.W. Cracker, loves geography lessons best of all. He dreams of visiting faraway lands. One day he packs a backpack and flies off on a trip around the world. As he travels, he writes letters describing the places he goes and his adventures to his school pals.

Key Vocabulary

canal	ferry	pyramid
chopsticks	freighter	sphinx
Chunnel	luggage	Stonehenge
dock	port	tourist
English Channel	preen	

Objectives

Reading Strategy—Genre: Recognizing humorous fiction
Language Skill: Identifying adverbs
Phonics/Word Study: Identifying words with *ew, ui, au, aw, al*
For more phonics practice, see *Steck-Vaughn Phonics* Level C, Unit 4, pages 109–112.

Our World of Wonders

The maps, text, and photographs of this nonfiction book take readers to the landscapes and landmarks of eight countries.

Glossary Words

architect	fertile	landscape
border	festival	monument
capital	geography	myth
custom	gondola	peninsula
czar	isolated	sculptor
exotic	landmark	temple

Other Key Vocabulary

column	Maya
dome	mountain range
justice	quetzal
macaw	

Objectives

Reading Strategy—Study Skills: Using maps
Language Skill: Identifying proper nouns and adjectives
Phonics/Word Study: Recognizing suffixes *-ous, -er, -or, -ist*
For more word study practice, see *Steck-Vaughn Phonics* Level C, Unit 6, pages 171–172.

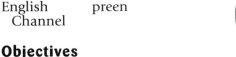

Additional Components

Audio Cassette: *P.W. Cracker Sees the World/ Our World of Wonders*
Writing Masters, pages 105–108
Take Me Home package

Other Resources About Geography

Jamaica Sandwich, Brian P. Cleary
Postcards from…, Steck-Vaughn
Many Places, Friendly Faces CD-ROM, Steck-Vaughn

P.W. Cracker Sees the World

BEFORE READING

Display the cover and invite a volunteer to read the title. Encourage students to guess who P.W. Cracker is. Explain that a landmark is a well-known building or structure of historical value, such as the Statue of Liberty. Have students read the table of contents on page 2 and predict the famous landmarks P.W. visits in chapters 2–6. Write students' responses on the board.

READING

To set a purpose for reading, ask students to find out the different ways P.W. travels as he journeys around the world. Use questions such as these to guide the reading:

- *What things does P.W. learn about the countries he visits? (chapters 2–6)*
- *What problems does P.W. encounter in his travels? (chapters 2–6)*
- *How does P.W. resolve these problems? (chapters 2–6)*
- *What clues let you know that this is a fiction book? (chapters 1–7)*

AFTER READING

Have volunteers read the list of places they made in Before Reading. Have them suggest additions or changes to the places as needed. Then have students make a flow chart on the board to show the ways in which P.W. travels.

Writing Activities

Letter Home
Materials: world map, encyclopedia or atlas

Have students imagine that P.W. went to a sixth country on his journey. Have them choose a place by looking on a world map and research information about the place. Invite students to write a letter from P.W. to the class describing one or more of the landmarks there. Display letters on a class bulletin board for other groups to read.

Our Pet's Travels
Materials: none

Write a class story about your class pet's imaginary world travels. If you do not have a class pet, tell students to pretend that you have a gerbil. With students decide which countries your pet will visit and the order in which the pet will travel. Then have small groups research assigned countries and use the facts they find to write about the pet's visit to the country. Remind students to include the way the pet travels.

■ READING STRATEGY

Genre: Recognizing Humorous Fiction

Point out that although there are many facts in this book, the story is humorous fiction. Explain that the purpose of humorous fiction is to entertain readers by making them laugh. Ask students to identify parts of the book that they think are funny. Invite students to think of other examples of humorous fiction.

■ LANGUAGE SKILL

Identifying Adverbs

Write *Soon P.W. was on a plane* and *P.W. glided silently down* on the board. Explain that adverbs are words that tell how, when, or where something happens. Point out that adverbs telling how usually end in –*ly*, such as *quickly* and *softly*. Help students to identify the adverbs in the sentences. Invite students to look through the story for other adverbs.

PHONICS/WORD STUDY

Identifying Words with *ew, ui, au, aw, al*

Explain that letter combinations containing vowels may have a short vowel sound, a long vowel sound, or a different vowel sound altogether. Point out that letters *ew* and *ui* can stand for the vowel sound in *flew* and *fruit* and that the letters *au, aw,* and *al* can stand for the vowel sound in *saucer, saw,* and *walk*. Have students look through the book to find examples of these letter combinations.

Our World of Wonders

BEFORE READING

Discuss famous people-made landmarks, such as Mount Rushmore and the Statue of Liberty. Then ask students to examine the cover and table of contents of the book and predict the famous landmarks they will read about. Have them write their predictions and revise their list as they read.

READING

To set a purpose for reading, ask students to read to learn one fact about each landmark in the book. Use questions such as the following to guide the reading:

- *How are the countries in the book alike? (chapters 1–8)*
- *How are the countries different? (chapters 1–8)*
- *What is the difference between a landscape and a landmark? (chapters 1–8)*
- *Which countries are peninsulas? (chapters 3, 5)*
- *Which chapter is about an island? (chapter 8)*

AFTER READING

Return to the list students made in Before Reading. Ask students to share their predictions and their findings with the class.

Writing Activities

Picture Postcards
Materials: large index cards, colored pencils, 1/2″ wide ribbon, glue

Ask partners to choose three countries from the book and create a picture postcard for each. Students should draw a picture of a famous landmark on one side of a large index card. On the other side, they should mark off a gap in the middle where they will glue the card to a long piece of ribbon. Students should then use the remaining space to write about the picture. Help partners glue their cards to long pieces of ribbon, one under the other. Hang the postcards for students to admire.

Travel Plan
Materials: travel books, country maps, Internet access (optional)

Have groups choose a country from the book that they might like to visit. You may wish to allow students to also select countries not in the book. Tell groups to plan a two-week visit to the country. Groups should write their travel plan, including how long they would stay at each town or city and what they would do. Remind groups to include landmarks they would like to see.

■ READING STRATEGY

Study Skills: Using Maps

Explain that maps are drawings that show where places are. Tell students that some maps show a large area and others show a smaller area. Also point out that some maps show cities, mountains, and rivers. Have students look at page 12. Explain how the world map and country map are related. Point out the features identified on the country map. Then ask students to turn to page 24 and discuss the two maps.

■ LANGUAGE SKILL

Identifying Proper Nouns and Adjectives

Explain to students that proper nouns name specific people, places, or things and that proper adjectives are made from proper nouns. Remind students that both are capitalized. On the board write *Hercules is a hero in many Greek myths.* Have students identify the proper noun and adjective. Then invite students to find other proper nouns and adjectives in the book.

PHONICS/WORD STUDY

Recognizing Suffixes *-ous*, *-er*, *-or*, *-ist*

Remind students that a suffix changes the meaning of a base word. Write *nervous, farmer, editor,* and *scientist* on the board and underline the suffixes *-ous*, *-er*, *-or*, and *-ist*. Explain that the suffix *-ous* means "full of," and the suffixes *-er*, *-or*, and *-ist* mean "a person who." Have students use the suffix meanings to define each word on the board. Then ask students to look for examples of each suffix in the book.

Tying the Pair Together

Display the two books and ask students how the books are alike and different. Invite students to tell what they learned about places around the world. Write their ideas on a language experience chart. Invite volunteers to take turns reading the chart aloud to the class.

Social Studies: Country Comparison
Materials: chart paper, encyclopedias

Have students make a chart comparing the countries in both books. Have them write the place names down the left side of the chart. Across the top they should write these headings: *Landmarks, Weather/ Climate, Landscape, Other Information.* Groups can then use the chart information to write sentences to compare and contrast two countries at a time.

Mathematics: How Far Is It?
Materials: world map with distance scale, ruler, calculator (optional)

Have partners use the distance scale on a world map to determine the number of miles or kilometers between countries in the books. Have students list the distances and then use the list to make up word problems, such as *We sailed from England to France and then from France to Egypt. How many miles did we travel?* and *How many more miles is it from France to Egypt than from England to France?* Have partners exchange lists and answer each other's questions.

Drama: How Did They Do It?
Materials: encyclopedias, information books

Help students research what is known about how the landmarks in the book were made. Then have students take roles and act out the construction. For landmarks for which there is little or no information, suggest that students make up something that could have really happened.

Creative Arts: Travel Poster
Materials: posterboard, markers or colored pencils, two-language dictionaries (optional)

Invite students to create a travel poster for one of the countries they have learned about. Have them try to convince visitors to come to the country by telling about its amazing landmarks. If possible, provide two-language dictionaries and have students add terms from the language spoken in the country, such as *bonjour* or *ciao.*

ASSESSMENT

- Have students describe one or two of the countries in either of the books.
- Provide students with humorous fiction and other types of fiction and have them identify the humorous fiction.
- Display a map and ask students to find specific mountains, rivers, or cities on it.
- Review samples of students' writings to assess comprehension of what they read.
- Use informal conferencing with students to assess comprehension and skill growth.

For further assessment see the checklist on pages 109–111.

Home Activities

Copy and distribute to students the *Take It Home* activity master on page 79 (English) or page 80 (Spanish). Invite students to describe to family members some landmarks they read about.

Dear Family of _____ ,

GEOGRAPHY ACTIVITIES

Your child has been reading about places around the world. In the whimsical tale *P.W. Cracker Sees the World*, a class parrot visits foreign countries. In the nonfiction companion book, *Our World of Wonders*, readers journey to eight countries with famous landmarks. To help your child learn more about places around the world, choose from the activities below.

GEOGRAPHY BOOKS

Help your child learn more about geography by visiting the library. Spend some time looking at an atlas such as *First Atlas* by Rand McNally and Company. Check out books such as *Blast Off to Earth!: A Look at Geography* by Loreen Leedy.

MOVIES AND MORE

Share videos about places near and far with your child. View movies such as *A Far Off Place* and *The Jungle Book* or travel films such Al Roker's film series *Going Places*.

You and your child can also view photographs of famous places in the gallery of The Travel Channel's Internet site (www.travelchannel.com).

ARTS AND CRAFTS: My Part of the World

Materials: poster paper, watercolor paints, brushes

Discuss with your child the landscape and landmarks in your community or town. Then invite your child to paint a picture showing what P.W. Cracker might see or eat if he came to your community or town. Help your child make up a title for the painting.

SHARE

Find a world map and encourage your child to locate places he or she hears or reads about. Each time your child locates a new place, ask a question such as *What mountain range is in this country?* or *What kind of climate do you think this country has?*

Estimada familia de _____,

ACTIVIDADES DE GEOGRAFÍA

Su niño/a ha estado leyendo acerca de lugares alrededor del mundo. En el juguetón cuento *P.W. Cracker Sees the World,* el loro de una clase visita países extranjeros. En el libro compañero de no es ficción, *Our World of Wonders,* los lectores visitan ocho países con famosos lugares de interés. Escoja de las actividades que siguen para ayudar a su niño/a a aprender más sobre lugares alrededor del mundo.

LIBROS DE GEOGRAFÍA

Ayúdele a su niño/a a aprender más visitando la biblioteca. Pasen un rato mirando un atlas tal como el *First Atlas* por Rand McNally y compañía. Saquen prestado libros tales como *Blast Off to Earth!: A Look at Geography* por Loreen Leedy.

PELÍCULAS Y MÁS

Comparta videos sobre lugares cercanos y distantes con su niño/a. Vean películas tales como *A Far Off Place* y *The Jungle Book* o la serial de películas de viajes como *Going Places* por Al Roker.

Usted y su niño/a pueden ver también fotografías de lugares famosos en la galería de The Travel Channel en el internet (www.travelchannel.com).

ARTE Y ARTESANÍA: Mi parte del mundo

Materiales: papel de cartel, acuarela, pinceles

Converse con su niño/a acerca del paisaje y lugares de interés en su comunidad o pueblo. Luego invite a su niño/a a pintar un cuadro que muestre lo que vería o comería P.W. Cracker si viniera a su comunidad o pueblo. Ayúdele a ponerle un título al cuadro.

COMPARTAN

Busque un mapa mundial y estimule a su niño/a a ubicar lugares sobre los cuales él o ella haya escuchado o leído algo. Cada vez que su niño/a ubique un nuevo lugar, pregúntele cosas como: *¿Qué cadena de montañas está en este país?* o *¿Qué clase de clima crees que tiene este país?*

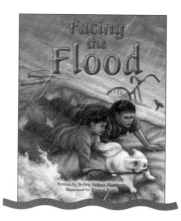

INTRODUCING THE PAIR-IT BOOKS

To introduce the topic of nature's forces, display the covers of *Facing the Flood* and *Nature's Power*. Have students read the titles and compare the covers. Ask students to use the covers to brainstorm a list of natural phenomena that can change the shape of our world and affect people's lives. Help students begin to see the forces of nature (wind, water, temperature, and gravity) that create these phenomena.

Facing the Flood

In this work of realistic fiction, a boy and his older sister are swept down a rushing creek. Alone and frightened, the two must use their wits and courage to make their way out of the crisis.

Key Vocabulary

bank (creek)	emergency	soggy
current	flood-prone	surge
debris	gush	survive
doubt	monstrous	zigzag
drizzle	raging	

Objectives

Reading Strategy—Comprehension: Predicting outcomes
Language Skill: Understanding dialogue
Phonics/Word Study: Identifying the sounds of *oo*
For more phonics practice, see *Steck-Vaughn Phonics* Level C, Unit 4, pages 107–108.

Nature's Power

Nature's awesome forces—wind, water, temperature, and gravity—are explored in this work of nonfiction.

Glossary Words

avalanche	glacier	sand dune
blizzard	magma	sinkhole
erupt	pumice	slipface
fault line	quicksand	tsunami
geyser	Richter scale	

Other Key Vocabulary

cyclone	typhoon
hot spring	waterspout
lava	

Objectives

Reading Strategy—Study Skills: Interpreting tables
Language Skill: Using commas in a series
Phonics/Word Study: Identifying compound words
For more word study practice, see *Steck-Vaughn Phonics* Level C, Unit 5, pages 125–126 and 135–136.

Additional Components

Audio Cassette: *Facing the Flood/Nature's Power*
Writing Masters, pages 105–108

Other Resources About Nature's Forces

Earthquake!, Steck-Vaughn
Ben's Dream, Chris Van Allsburg
Earth: Forces and Formations CD-ROM, Steck-Vaughn

Facing the Flood

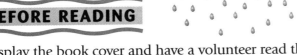

BEFORE READING

Display the book cover and have a volunteer read the title. Explain that in a flash flood, very heavy rain causes creeks, rivers, and other bodies of water to rise rapidly and often to overflow. Have students predict what might happen to land and people in a flash flood. Write their predictions on the board.

READING

To set a purpose for reading, ask students to find out how the flood affects Jesse and his family. Use questions such as these to guide the reading:

- *What problems does the storm cause? (chapters 1–6)*
- *How do Sara and Jesse try to protect themselves once they are in the creek? (chapters 3–4)*
- *How do Sara and Jesse escape from the creek? (chapter 4)*
- *How does a flash flood affect people and property? (chapters 3–6)*

AFTER READING

Have volunteers read their predictions made in Before Reading. Ask if their predictions were disproved or confirmed. Also ask what Jesse discovered to be really important *(his family, including Scooter)*.

Writing Activities

Story Response Journal
Materials: construction paper, colored pencils

Have students staple several sheets of paper inside a construction paper cover to make a story-response journal. Invite students to use the journal to describe Jesse. Have them write what happens to him, how he feels, and how he changes as the story progresses. Encourage students to illustrate their journal and share it with each other.

All the News
Materials: none

Invite partners to take roles, one as a newspaper reporter and the other as Jesse or Sara, one of the characters in the story. Have the reporter interview the character, asking questions about the flood and the adventure. Encourage reporters to ask who, what, when, where, why, and how questions. Then have partners work together to write a newspaper article about the Reyna children's ordeal.

MINI LESSONS

■ READING STRATEGY
Comprehension: Predicting Outcomes

Explain that guessing what happens in a book before we read it can help us understand it better. Tell students that the chapter titles, text, and pictures can tell us about a book's content. Ask students whether *Facing the Flood* could have had a different outcome. Then ask students to predict an outcome for the story if the rain had stopped before the creek banks overflowed.

■ LANGUAGE SKILL
Understanding Dialogue

Read the fourth paragraph on page 3 aloud with expression. Direct students' attention to the quotation marks and the word *scolded*. Explain that these clues indicate that a character is speaking. Point out that the word *scolded* tells how Jesse is speaking. Change the word to *whispered* and read the quotation aloud again. Have students work with partners to find other dialogue in the story. Encourage them to take turns reading the quotations aloud with meaning.

PHONICS/WORD STUDY

Identifying the Sounds of *oo*

Write the words *look* and *Scooter* on the board and have a volunteer read them. Ask students how the words are alike and different *(both have oo, but the sounds of oo are different)*. Explain that the vowel digraph *oo* can stand for both sounds. Invite students to brainstorm other words with *oo* and write them on the board under the word with the same vowel sound. Have volunteers read the lists aloud.

NATURE'S POWER

BEFORE READING

Have students read the book's title and examine the cover photograph and interior visuals. Invite volunteers to relate their experiences with nature's forces. Make a two-column chart on the board with *Cause* and *Effect* as headings. In the *Cause* column write *water, wind, temperature,* and *gravity.* Have students guess or tell what effects each force might cause. For example, they might write *floods* as an effect of the force of water.

READING

To set a purpose for reading, ask students to find out how nature's forces change the land. Use questions such as these to guide the reading:

- *What good things do wind and water cause? (chapters 2–3, 5)*
- *What are some of the problems caused by tsunamis, tornadoes, earthquakes, and volcanoes? (chapters 2–5)*
- *How are typhoons, cyclones, and hurricanes similar and different? (chapter 3)*
- *Would you rather visit a glacier, a sand dune, or a geyser? Why? (chapter 6)*

AFTER READING

Return to the cause/effect chart made in Before Reading. Invite students to add facts they learned from the book.

Writing Activities

Dear Pen Pal
Materials: colored pencils (optional), envelopes (optional)

Have students pretend to live near places where natural phenomena occur, such as near the sand dunes in Colorado or near a volcano in Hawaii. Tell students to write letters to each other describing where they live. Students should write what they like and dislike about living where they do. Some students may want to illustrate their letter or address an envelope and "mail" the letter to their partner.

Nature's Forces at Work
Materials: 9" X 12" drawing paper, colored pencils

Have students fold the paper into fourths or eighths. Have students draw "snapshots" showing how one or more natural forces can change one particular place. For example, they may draw *before, during,* and *after* pictures of a flash flood or volcano. Students should write captions below each picture. Invite students to share their snapshots.

■ READING STRATEGY

Study Skills: Interpreting Tables

Direct students' attention to the table on page 27. Have them read the title and the column headings. Explain that creating a table is a way to organize information and that tables can help people understand information quickly. Have partners take turns asking each other questions about the table on page 27, such as *Where was the strongest earthquake?*

■ LANGUAGE SKILL

Using Commas in a Series

Write *Floods can ruin farmland, homes, roads, and neighborhoods* on the board. Explain that when three or more things occur in a row, they form a series and that commas are used to separate them. Invite partners to write sentences with series. Students can exchange sentences and punctuate the series correctly.

PHONICS/WORD STUDY

Identifying Compound Words

Write *earthquake* on the board and explain that it is a compound word because it is made up of two words. Have a volunteer draw a line between *earth* and *quake.* Provide several words from the book, such as *yourself, farmland, snowflake, snowfall, destroy, landform, mountain, roaring,* and *thunderstorm.* Have partners identify the compound words and the two words from which they are made.

Tying the Pair Together

Display *Facing the Flood* and *Nature's Power* and ask students how the books are alike and different. Invite volunteers to tell what they learned about nature's power. Then have students write sentences to describe one force of nature. Allow them to refer to the books as needed.

Music: Swirling, Twirling Typhoon

Invite students to sing along as you sing "The Bear Went over the Mountain." Then invite students to make up new verses to the song, using the forces of nature. For example, they might use the words *sailor* and *ocean* in the first verse instead of *bear* and *mountain*, and they might change the third verse as follows:

A twirling, swirling typhoon,
A twirling, swirling typhoon,
A twirling, swirling typhoon,
Was all that he could see.

Social Studies: Game of Forces
Materials: index cards, colored pencils

Have students list several natural phenomena such as volcanoes or avalanches. For each word students should make two cards that include a picture and a description. Mix up the cards and place them facedown on a table. Students should try to make matches by turning over cards. When students make a match, they read the name of the phenomenon and tell what forces are involved.

Drama: A Helping Hand
Materials: none

Have partners pretend to be relief workers on site after a volcanic eruption, an avalanche, a flash flood, a tornado, or a tsunami. Have partners act out what they would do and say about the event. Encourage them to describe what they see, smell, hear, and feel.

Science: Forces Face-off
Materials: none

Have partners face each other. Ask partners a question such as *How can water change the shape of Earth?* Give each partner a few minutes to think about his or her answer. Then have each partner take a turn stating and explaining his or her answer. Remind students to listen carefully and think about how their answers are alike and different. Encourage partners to ask each other questions to clarify an answer.

ASSESSMENT

- Ask students to retell a part of *Facing the Flood*. Then have students describe how a force of nature can be gentle and dangerous.
- Have students preview a short book or magazine article and predict what it is about.
- Display a table of information and ask students questions about it.
- Review samples of students' writings to assess comprehension of what they read.
- Use informal conferencing with students to assess comprehension and skill growth.

For further assessment see the checklist on pages 109–111.

Home Activities

Copy and distribute to students the *Take It Home* activity master on page 85 (English) or page 86 (Spanish). Invite students to ask family members to discuss natural phenomena they have heard about or experienced.

TAKE IT HOME

Dear Family of _____ ,

ACTIVITIES ABOUT NATURE'S POWER

Your child has been reading about the power of nature's forces. In *Facing the Flood*, a boy and his teenage sister are swept down a flooding creek. The companion book, *Nature's Power*, describes the many different forces that shape our world, such as wind, water, and temperature. To help your child learn more about nature's power, choose from the activities below.

BOOKS ABOUT NATURE'S POWER

Help your child learn more about the forces of nature by visiting the library. Check out *How Mountains are Made* by Kathleen Weidner Zoehfeld and *I'll Know What to Do: A Kid's Guide to Natural Disasters* by Bonnie S. Mark.

MOVIES AND MORE

Look for documentary films about avalanches, tornadoes, volcanoes, and hurricanes. Encourage your child's interest in natural phenomena by watching videos of the Discovery Channel's *Raging Planet* series. Talk with your child about the forces at work in the natural phenomena.

ARTS AND CRAFTS: Power Plate

Materials: 2 paper plates, colored pencils or markers, scissors, brad

Draw lines to divide a paper plate into four equal sections. Ask your child to draw a picture in each section to show nature's power. On a second plate, have your child cut out a section the same size as one on the first plate. Place the second plate on top of the first and use the brad to fasten them together at their center. Ask your child to turn the top plate, reveal a picture, and tell something about it.

SHARE

Look for news reports on TV, in newspapers, or on the Internet that tell about the effects of a tornado, flood, hurricane, avalanche, or other natural phenomenon. Discuss with your child how the phenomenon changed the land and the lives of the residents.

Estimada familia de _____,

ACTIVIDADES ACERCA DE LA FUERZA DE LA NATURALEZA

Su niño/a ha estado leyendo acerca de la fuerza de la naturaleza. En *Facing the Flood*, un niño con su hermana adolescente son arrastrados a una quebrada que se inundaba. El libro compañero, *Nature's Power*, describe las diferentes fuerzas que forman nuestro mundo, tales como el viento, el agua y la temperatura. Para ayudarle a su niño/a a aprender más acerca de los poderes de la naturaleza, escoja de las actividades que siguen.

LIBROS ACERCA DE LA FUERZA DE LA NATURALEZA

Ayúdele a su niño/a a aprender más acerca de la fuerza de la naturaleza visitando la biblioteca. Saquen prestado *How Mountains Are Made* por Kathleen Weidner Zoehfeld y *I'll Know What to Do: A Kid's Guide to Natural Disasters* por Bonnie S. Mark.

PELÍCULAS Y MÁS

Busquen documentales sobre avalanchas, tornados, volcanes y huracanes. Estimule el interés de su niño/a en los fenómenos naturales mirando videos en el Discovery Channel en la serie *Raging Planet*. Conversen acerca de las fuerzas en juego en los fenómenos naturales.

ARTE Y ARTESANÍA: Plato de poder

Materiales: 2 platos de papel, lápices de colores o marcadores, tijeras, puntilla (brad)

Dibujen líneas para dividir un plato de papel en cuatro secciones iguales. Pídale a su niño/a que dibuje un cuadro en cada sección para mostrar la fuerza de la naturaleza. En el segundo plato, pídale a su niño/a que recorte una sección del mismo tamaño que las secciones del primer plato. Coloquen el segundo plato sobre el primero y usen la puntilla para sujetarlos por el centro. Pídale a su niño/a que gire el plato que está encima, que muestre un dibujo y que diga algo sobre el dibujo.

COMPARTAN

Busquen reportajes de noticias en la television, en periódicos o en el internet que hable sobre los efectos de un tornado, inundación, huracán, avalancha u otro fenómeno natural. Conversen sobre cómo el fenómeno cambió el terreno y las vidas de sus residentes.

INTRODUCING THE PAIR-IT BOOKS

To introduce the topic of codes, write the message *DPEFT BSF GVO.* Tell students that this message is *CODES ARE FUN* (See *All About Codes,* page 16, for the cipher key). Then display copies of the two books; identify the first as realistic fiction and the second as a nonfiction book.

Casey's Code

Young Casey loves to sail with her grandfather, but doesn't share his enthusiasm for Morse code. She thinks it's too old-fashioned until a sudden storm at sea teaches her the value of those little dots and dashes.

Key Vocabulary

cargo	key	plotted (a course)
compass	pierce	shuddered
despair	porthole	
gangway		

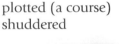

Objectives

Reading Strategy—Literary: Understanding conflicts and resolutions
Language Skill: Identifying adjectives
Phonics/Word Study: Identifying syllables with vowels sounded alone
For more phonics practice, see *Steck-Vaughn Phonics* Level C, Unit 5, pages 141–142.

All About Codes

This entertaining information book begins with early writing systems and ends with directions for making a simple cipher machine. Along the way students will learn about many codes and message systems: Morse code, Braille, sign language, bar codes, and more.

Glossary Words

Braille	cuneiform	pictograph
cipher	decode	scribe
cipher key	encode	semaphore
code	hieroglyphics	shorthand
communicate	Morse code	signal
complicated		

Other Key Vocabulary

gesture	substitution
sign	telegraph

Objectives

Reading Strategy—Comprehension: Applying information
Language Skill: Understanding acronyms
Phonics/Word Study: Recognizing prefixes
   de-, in-, im-, re-
For more word study practice, see *Steck-Vaughn Phonics* Level C, Unit 6, pages 173–176.

Additional Components

Audio Cassette: *Casey's Code/All About Codes*
Writing Masters, pages 105–108

Other Resources About Codes

Codes for Kids, Burton Albert
Pass It On!, Sharon Bailly
The Secret Code Book, Helen Huckle

Casey's CODE

BEFORE READING

Have students brainstorm ways they might call for help in an emergency and list their suggestions on the board. Discuss the book title and cover, and then tell students that there is an emergency in this book. Then preview several illustrations and call on volunteers to predict what the emergency is.

READING

To set a purpose for reading, ask students to read to find out the problem that Casey and her grandfather have. Use questions such as these to guide the reading:

- *What's bothering Casey when she first boards* Sun Sailor? *(chapter 1)*
- *How does Casey feel about Morse code at the beginning of the story? (chapters 1–3)*
- *How does Casey's opinion of herself change? (chapters 1–6)*
- *How does Casey get help? (chapter 6)*

AFTER READING

Call on volunteers to describe how Casey's feelings about herself and about Morse code change.

Writing Activities

Recognizing Sensory Language

The author uses vivid language to let readers know how Casey experiences the sudden storm. We learn what she sees, hears, feels, and even tastes. Have partners make a chart with the headings *See, Hear, Feel,* and *Taste.* Then ask students to reread pages 24–28 to find words and phrases for each category.

Morse Code
Materials: encyclopedia

Help groups of interested students locate copies of international Morse code in an encyclopedia. Then have each group write another story set on a boat or ship. Tell students to have the characters in the story send or receive a message in Morse code. Possible messages include *Send food, I'm lost,* and *My leg is hurt.* Groups can exchange and read each other's story.

MINI LESSONS

■ READING STRATEGY

Literary: Understanding Conflicts and Resolutions

Explain that often characters in stories have conflicts that are worked out by the end of the story. Call on volunteers to identify the conflicts in the story *(Casey's inner conflict about her abilities and Casey's conflict with the storm).* Then read aloud the last paragraph of the story. Discuss with students how these conflicts are resolved.

■ LANGUAGE SKILL

Identifying Adjectives

Tell students that an adjective describes a noun by answering questions such as *Which one? What kind? How many?* or *How much?* Read this sentence aloud and model how to identify the adjectives: *Brilliant streaks of lightning raced across the dark sky.* Write *streaks* on the board and suggest other adjectives to describe streaks of lightning, for example, *long, jagged, frightening.* Repeat with other sentences.

PHONICS/WORD STUDY

Identifying Syllables with Vowels Sounded Alone

Write these words from the story, without underlining, on the board and say them aloud with students: *even, ocean, United, electric, radio, aboard, family, apart.* Repeat each word slowly, emphasizing its syllables, and have volunteers draw vertical lines to divide the words into syllables. Point out that when a vowel is sounded alone in a word, it forms a syllable by itself. Repeat the procedure with these words: *emergency, okay, America, across.*

ALL ABOUT CODES

BEFORE READING

Have students preview *All About Codes* by reading the chapter titles and examining several pictures. Explain that this book is about special kinds of communication. Write *What We Know About Codes*, *What We Want to Know About Codes*, and *What We Learned About Codes* as column headings on the board. Invite students to contribute ideas for the first column.

READING

To help students set a purpose for reading, have them closely examine the pictures and captions and then write questions they hope will be answered. Have students add these questions to the chart they began in Before Reading. Also use questions such as these to guide the reading:

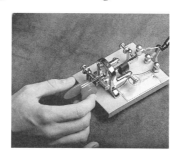

- *What are some different ways of communicating? (chapters 1–5)*
- *How is a code different from a cipher? (chapter 3)*
- *What are three tips for breaking ciphers and codes? (chapter 4)*
- *What does a cipher machine do? (chapter 5)*

AFTER READING

Call students' attention to the chart on the board. Ask them what they learned about codes and write their responses in the appropriate column.

Writing Activities

Informational Posters
Materials: poster paper, markers, reference books

Invite pairs of students to make a poster that graphically presents a code, cipher, or other message system. Each poster should include a message encoded by using the system.

Demonstrating Sign Language
Materials: information books about sign language, note cards

Invite interested students to form a small group to study sign language and to learn several signs. Then have students write a short report about sign language. Students should read their report aloud and demonstrate some signs that they learned.

MINI LESSONS

■ READING STRATEGY
Comprehension: Applying Information
Tell students that some books, such as school workbooks, craft books, and cookbooks explain how to do things. Then help students use the tips on pages 30–31 to decode the message on page 32. (The answer is on page 40.)

■ LANGUAGE SKILL
Understanding Acronyms
Write *ATM* and *PIN* on the board, and explain that *ATM* means "automated teller machine" and *PIN* means "personal identification number." Then help students figure out the acronyms for these phrases: *save our ship (SOS), zone improvement plan (ZIP), very important person (VIP), television (TV), tender loving care (TLC), bacon, lettuce, and tomato sandwich (BLT), recreational vehicle (RV).*

PHONICS/WORD STUDY

Recognizing Prefixes *de-, in-, im-, re-*

Explain that a prefix is a word part added to the beginning of a base word to change its meaning. Write *decode, defrost, invisible, incomplete, impossible, impatient, replace,* and *redial* on the board and underline the prefixes. For each word, create pairs of sentences such as *The spy knew the message was written in code. She quickly decoded it.* Afterward, explain that the prefixes *in-* and *im-* mean "not," *de-* means "to remove," and *re-* means "again."

Tying the Pair Together

Work with students to develop a Venn diagram that compares the fiction book *Casey's Code* with the information book *All About Codes*. Encourage students to express opinions about why they might choose to read each type of book.

Drama: Mixed Words
Materials: large index cards, markers, timer

Divide the class into two teams. Have each meet secretly to think of three words from *Casey's Code,* such as *code, gangway,* and *storm.* Students should write the words, one letter per index card. To play, Team 1 displays a word along the chalk rail, mixing up the letters within each word. Team 2 has three minutes to decode the word and rearrange the letters correctly.

Social Studies: Grocery Code
Materials: none

Remind students that codes are sometimes used for simplicity instead of secrecy. For example, the two-letter state codes simplify mail delivery. Have students think of several ways codes could be used to simplify a grocery list. For example, *ban* could stand for *bananas,* and *pb* could stand for *peanut butter.* Encourage groups to share their code.

Mathematics: Shapes Code
Materials: none

Challenge students to solve problems you make up in which shapes stand for numbers. You'll need both an addition and subtraction clue for each problem. Students must figure out what the $\square$ and Δ stand for. Here are three examples:

$\square + \Delta = 9; \square - \Delta = 3$

$\square + \Delta = 13; \square - \Delta = 7$

$\square + \Delta = 9; \square - \Delta = 1$

Creative Arts: Cipher Machine
Materials: soda cans, white paper

Organize students into teams of three. Have each team make a cipher machine as described on page 38 and use it to encode a message. Have teams then trade machines and messages and decode the messages.

ASSESSMENT

- Ask students to retell the story of *Casey's Code* and to summarize the information in *All About Codes.*
- Observe whether students can identify a conflict and resolution in a work of fiction.
- Note whether students can use the ciphers in *All About Codes* to encode and decode messages.
- Review samples of students' writings to assess comprehension of what they read.
- Use informal conferencing with students to assess comprehension and skill growth.

For further assessment see the checklist on pages 109–111.

Home Activities

Copy and distribute to students the *Take It Home* activity master on page 91 (English) or on page 92 (Spanish). Invite students to discuss with their families the facts they have learned about codes.

TAKE IT HOME

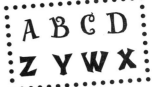

Dear Family of _____,

CODE ACTIVITIES

Your child has been reading about the intriguing subject of codes and ciphers. A fiction book called *Casey's Code* shows how a young girl's knowledge of Morse code saves her grandfather's life. A nonfiction selection, *All About Codes*, provides details about message systems used throughout history and shows how to make up simple codes and ciphers.

BOOKS ABOUT CODES

Help your child learn more about codes and ciphers by visiting the library. Look for the information books *Codes* by Nigel Nelson, *Pass It On!* by Sharon Bailly, and *The Secret Code Book* by Helen Huckle.

MOVIES AND MORE

With your child look for these videos at the library or video rental store: *Pee Wee's Big Adventure*, which demonstrates how Morse code can be used, and *Look What I Found: Making Codes and Solving Mysteries*.

ARTS AND CRAFTS: Cipher Greeting Card

Materials: unlined paper, envelope, colored markers

With your child create a cipher key by printing the alphabet in order on a long strip of paper. Then print the alphabet in reverse order under the original letters. Fold a sheet of paper in half to make a greeting card. On the inside write a message by using letters in the second set to stand for letters in the first. Decorate the outside of the card. Be sure to send along the cipher key for decoding the message.

SHARE

Codes are part of everyday life. Go on a scavenger hunt for different types of codes in your home. Look for area codes in phone books, state codes on envelopes, and bar codes on food boxes. Talk with your child about how each code is used.

Estimada familia de _____,

ACTIVIDADES DE CÓDIGOS

Su niño/a ha estado leyendo acerca del intrigante tema de los códigos y cifras. Un libro de ficción llamado *Casey's Code* muestra cómo el conocimiento de una joven del código Morse le salva la vida al abuelo. Una selección de no ficción, *All About Codes*, proporciona detalles sobre los sistemas de mensajes usados a través de la historia y enseña cómo hacer cifras y códigos simples.

LIBROS ACERCA DE CÓDIGOS

Ayúdele a su niño/a a aprender más sobre códigos y cifras visitando la biblioteca. Busquen los libros de información *Codes* por Nigel Nelson, *Pass It On!* por Sharon Bailly y *The Secret Code Book* por Helen Huckle.

PELÍCULAS Y MÁS

Busquen estos videos en la biblioteca o en la tienda para alquilar videos: *Pee Wee's Big Adventure,* que demuestra cómo se puede usar el código Morse, y *Look What I Found: Making Codes and Solving Mysteries.*

ARTE Y ARTESANÍA: Tarjetas de felicitaciones en cifras

Materiales: papel sin líneas, sobre, marcadores de colores

Con su niño/a cree una clave de cifras imprimiendo el alfabeto en orden en una larga tira de papel. Luego impriman el alfabeto en orden inverso bajo las letras originales. Doble una hoja de papel por la mitad para hacer una tarjeta de felicitaciones. En el interior, escriba un mensaje usando letras del segundo grupo para que representen letras del primer grupo. Decoren la parte exterior de la tarjeta. Asegúrense de enviar también la clave de cifras para descifrar el mensaje.

COMPARTAN

Los códigos son parte de la vida cotidiana. Busquen diferentes tipos de códigos por toda la casa. Busquen códigos de área en el guía de teléfonos, códigos estatales en los sobres y códigos de barra en cajas de alimentos. Conversen sobre la forma cómo se usa cada código.

Szkkb
Yrkqswzb!

INTRODUCING THE PAIR-IT BOOKS

To introduce the topic of the universe, display the covers of *The Night Queen's Blue Velvet Dress* and *The Universe*. Call on a student to read aloud the titles. Explain that the first book is a story, and the other offers factual information. Invite students to generate a list of objects in the universe as you record them on the board. Then call on volunteers to underline the names of those in our solar system.

The Night Queen's Blue Velvet Dress

Leo is worried when his mother says he will spend a week with his grandmother in the Arizona desert, but his fears are soon laid to rest. The Arizona sky glitters with stars. And Nana, a taskmaster by day, becomes a magical storyteller by night. Leo is intrigued by her story of the Night Queen.

Key Vocabulary

accomplish	phases	reflect
constellation	planetarium	twinkling
gaze	protest	

Objectives

Reading Strategy—Literary: Understanding setting

Language Skill: Understanding compound predicates

Phonics/Word Study: Understanding sounds of *ou*

For more phonics practice, see *Steck-Vaughn Phonics* Level C, Unit 4, pages 113–114.

Additional Components

Audio Cassette: *The Night Queen's Blue Velvet Dress/ The Universe*

Writing Masters, pages 105–108

Take Me Home Package

The Universe

This book's text, photographs, Did You Know? features, and diagrams take students to our solar system and beyond. Chapters cover the sun, moon, nine planets of our solar system, stars, meteors, comets, and galaxies.

Glossary Words

asteroid	crater	orbit
atmosphere	galaxy	pole
comet	meteor	rotate
constellation	meteorite	solar eclipse
corona	meteoroid	solar system

Other Key Vocabulary

gorge	streak
halo	

Objectives

Reading Strategy—Study Skills: Using text features

Language Skill: Using antonyms

Phonics/Word Study: Recognizing suffixes *-en*, *-ous*, *-ion*

For more word study practice, see *Steck-Vaughn Phonics* Level C, Unit 6, pages 169–171.

Other Resources About the Universe

Comet in Moominland, Tove Jansson

What About . . . the Sun and Stars, Steck-Vaughn

Steck-Vaughn Interactive Science Encyclopedia CD-ROM

The Night Queen's Blue Velvet Dress

BEFORE READING

Call on a volunteer to read aloud the book title. Then have students examine the illustrations on pages 13 and 31. Explain that the book tells two stories—one about a boy and his grandmother and another about the Night Queen.

READING

Encourage students to set a purpose for reading. Call on a few volunteers to share their purpose. You may want to suggest that students read to find out all the things the Night Queen adds to her dress. Use questions such as the following to guide the reading:

- *What does Leo especially like about Nana and where she lives? (chapters 2 and 3)*
- *What happens at the start of the Night Queen story? (chapter 3)*
- *What do Leo's notebook entries tell about his feelings? (chapters 2–8)*
- *What does the Night Queen do with the blue velvet dress at the end of the story? Why? (chapter 8)*

AFTER READING

Call on volunteers to tell what they would like and dislike about a week with Nana at her desert house.

Writing Activities

Postcards to Mom
Materials: large index cards, markers or colored pencils

Have students imagine that at the end of each day with Nana, Leo sends a postcard to his mother. Have each student choose a day and reread that section of the book. Then have them compose a short message on one side of an index card and draw a picture on the reverse side. Students can then read the cards aloud in book order.

An Uncle Sun Tale
Materials: none

Have small groups of students make up a folktale featuring the sun. Remind students that the sun appears to move in the sky from east to west every day. Then give students this story starter: *For many years Uncle Sun had gotten up early every day and worked hard until it was dark. But this day was different. Uncle Sun . . . .* Tell groups to write the rest of the story. Encourage students to write stories that end with Uncle Sun returning to his normal daily activities.

MINI LESSONS

■ READING STRATEGY
Literary: Understanding Setting

Explain that *setting* is the term for when and where a story takes place. Tell students that this book has two settings and have volunteers describe them. Encourage students to find illustrations that depict the settings. Select other works of fiction and ask students to identify the setting of each.

■ LANGUAGE SKILL
Understanding Compound Predicates

Explain that all sentences have at least two parts: the subject, which names what the sentence is about, and the predicate, which tells what the subject is or does. Point out that the predicate includes the verb and may have more than one verb. Read aloud this sentence: *Leo stepped slowly out of the jeep and looked around.* Explain that *Leo* is the subject, and the rest of the sentence is a compound predicate because it has two verbs, *stepped* and *looked*. Have students use the story events to make up sentences with compound predicates.

PHONICS/WORD STUDY

Understanding Sounds of *ou*

Explain that the letters *ou* can stand for four different sounds. Say the words *thought, enough, four,* and *you.* Have students repeat the words and listen for the vowel sounds. Then write the words as headings on the board. Read aloud the following words and have students write each in the appropriate column: *pour, nervous, cough, gibbous, course, fought, soup, source, youth.* Ask students to look through the book and find other words to add to the columns.

The Universe

BEFORE READING

To help students preview the book, have students write *The Universe* at the top of a sheet of paper. Under it they should make a three-column chart with the headings *What I Know, What I Want to Learn,* and *What I Learned.* Discuss with students what they know and want to learn. Then give students a few minutes to write on their chart what they know and want to learn.

READING

Invite students to set a purpose for their reading. You might help by asking what they wonder about when they look at the night sky or when they hear news about space voyages. Use questions such as the following to guide the reading:

- *What causes the two types of eclipses? (chapter 2)*
- *Which two planets have rings? (chapter 7)*
- *Which planet has the most moons that we know about? (chapter 7)*

- *What are the differences between meteoroids, meteors, and meteorites? (chapter 10)*

AFTER READING

Give students a few minutes to review the book and decide which facts they find most interesting. Have them add these facts to the third column of the chart they began in Before Reading. Then have them complete the third column.

Writing Activities

Planet Descriptions
Materials: drawing paper, markers, encyclopedias, information books about the solar system

Have each student write and illustrate a paragraph comparing a chosen planet to Earth. Paragraphs might include information about the surfaces of the two planets, comparative size, number of moons, and distances from the sun.

Space Traveler
Materials: encyclopedias, information books, outer space background music (optional)

Have small groups write a science fiction adventure about a trip into space. Encourage students to include as many facts as possible. Remind students that the story should have a beginning, middle, and end. To spark students' creativity, you may want to play outer space background music.

MINI LESSONS

■ READING STRATEGY

Study Skills: Using Text Features

Explain that some information books contain special boxes with additional information. Have students turn to page 7. Have a volunteer read aloud the Did You Know? box. Then have students look for more Did You Know? boxes in the book. Call on students to share the information they learned from these special boxes.

■ LANGUAGE SKILL

Using Antonyms

Explain that antonyms are words that have opposite meanings and that writers sometimes use antonyms to point out a difference. Read aloud this sentence and then identify the antonyms: *The moon is very hot in some places and very cold in others.* Afterward work with students to make up sentences with these antonyms: *closest/farthest, always/never, huge/tiny, rough/smooth, sunrise/sunset.*

PHONICS/WORD STUDY

Recognizing Suffixes
-en, -ous, -ion

Explain that a suffix is a word part added to the end of a base word to change its meaning. Write *monstrous, poisonous, molten, darken, rotation,* and *eruption* on the board and underline the suffixes. Explain that *-ous* means "full of," *-en* means "to become," and *-ion* means "the act of" or "the result of an action." Then write *Io has 9 volcanoes that spew molten, poisonous sulfur about 60 miles straight up* and *The ice eruptions can spray across Triton for 100 miles.* Challenge students to define *molten, poisonous,* and *eruptions.*

Tying the Pair Together

Display the two books and ask students to share what they have learned about the unierse. Have students find the chapters and sections in *The Universe* that correspond to the decorations on the Night Queen's dress.

Language Arts: Sky Story
Materials: trade books

All cultures have myths and folktales to explain the mysterious night sky. Invite students to read tales from other cultures and choose their favorites to retell for classmates. Consider these books: *Moontellers: Myths of the Moon from Around the World* by Lynn Moroney; *Sacred Skies: The Facts and the Fables* by Finn Bevan; and *Sun, Moon, and Stars* by Mary Hoffman.

Creative Arts: Star Map
Materials: construction paper, colored markers, encyclopedias, information books

Have students create their own star map of the Northern Hemisphere so they can identify well-known constellations at night. Pages 32–33 of *The Universe* can be used as a reference. Encourage students to label the North Star (at the very top of Ursa Minor) and the constellations closest to it. Explain that at night all the star groups appear to rotate around the North Star. Invite interested students to use other sources of information to add other constellations to their star map.

Science: Careers in Space Science
Materials: Internet access

What do space scientists really do? How do they get their job? Students interested in learning about careers in space science can go on-line at Quest: NASA K–12 Internet Initiative (quest.arc.nasa.gov) and Space Scientists Online (quest.arc.nasa.gov/sso) and report their findings to the rest of the class.

Mathematics: Number Facts About the Universe
Materials: encyclopedias or almanacs, information books about space

Have small groups prepare and present selected number facts about the universe. For example, a group assigned the number 4 might present these facts: *It would take 4 moons to equal the size of Earth. There are 4 hard and rocky planets. Mars is the fourth planet from the sun.*

ASSESSMENT

- Ask students to give explanations for the appearance of the night sky from Nana's story and from *The Universe*.
- Ask students to describe the settings (time and place) of a few familiar stories.
- Have students find other selected special text features in other nonfiction books.
- Review samples of students' writing to assess comprehension of what they read.
- Use informal conferencing with students to assess comprehension and skill growth.

For further assessment see the checklist on pages 109–111.

Home Activities

Copy and distribute to students the *Take It Home* activity master on page 97 (English) or page 98 (Spanish). Invite students to discuss with their family the facts they have learned about the universe.

TAKE IT HOME

Dear Family of _____,

UNIVERSE ACTIVITIES

Your child has been reading about the universe. *The Night Queen's Blue Velvet Dress* is a story about a boy's visit to his grandmother, who weaves a tale under the star-filled Arizona skies. *The Universe* is a nonfiction book that introduces our solar system and other elements of the universe.

UNIVERSE BOOKS

Visit the library with your child and look for these information books: *Comets, Meteors, and Asteroids* by Seymour Simon and *The Magic School Bus Gets Lost in Space* by Lily Tomlin. For a good mystery, check out *The Outer Space Mystery* by Gertrude C. Warner.

MOVIES AND MORE

View movies and videos about outer space with your child. *The Magic School Bus Gets Lost in Space* provides information as well as entertainment. For great space fantasies, watch these award winning films: *E.T.—The Extra-Terrestrial* and *Star Wars*. Talk with your child about the elements of the universe featured in the films.

ARTS AND CRAFTS: What's in the Stars?

Materials: drawing paper, colored pencils or crayons, marker

With your child make a simple drawing or outline of an animal or object. For example, you might draw a turtle, pig, mouse, chair, car, or ladder. Imagine that the drawing represents a group of stars in the sky and add the stars to the drawing with a marker. Make a second drawing of another animal or object, this time beginning with stars. Then connect the stars to complete the drawing.

SHARE

The Earth's gravity keeps us and our possessions here on the ground. Encourage your child to tell or write a fanciful story about a day when the pull of gravity slowly fades away. Encourage vivid descriptions of the events that occur.

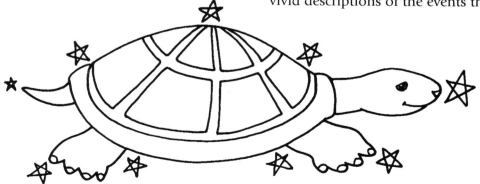

LLÉVAME A CASA

Estimada familia de _____,

ACTIVIDADES DEL UNIVERSO

Su niño/a ha estado leyendo sobre el universo. *The Night Queen's Blue Velvet Dress* es un cuento acerca de la visita que hace un niño a su abuela, quien teje un cuento bajo el cielo estrellado de Arizona. *The Universe*, un libro de no ficción, introduce nuestro sistema solar y otros elementos del universo.

LIBROS DEL UNIVERSO

Visite la biblioteca con su niño/a y busque estos libros de información: *Comets, Meteors, and Asteroids* por Seymour Simon y *The Magic School Bus Gets Lost in Space* por Lily Tomlin. Para leer un buen misterio, saque *The Outer Space Mystery* por Gertrude C. Warner.

PELÍCULAS Y MÁS

Vea películas y videos sobre el espacio con su niño/a. *The Magic School Bus Gets Lost in Space* proporciona información y también entretenimiento. Para grandes fantasías en el espacio, vea estas películas ganadoras de premios: *E.T—The Extra-Terrestrial* y *Star Wars*. Converse con su niño/a acerca de los elementos del universo que aparecen en las películas.

ARTE Y ARTESANÍA: ¿Qué hay en las estrellas?

Materiales: papel de dibujo, lápices de colores o creyones, marcador

Con su niño/a, haga un simple dibujo o el contorno de algún animal u objeto. Por ejemplo, podrían dibujar una tortuga, un cerdo, un raton, una silla, un automóvil o una escalera. Imaginen que el dibujo representa un grupo de estrellas en el cielo y agreguen estrellas al dibujo con un marcador. Hagan un segundo dibujo de otro animal u objeto, esta vez comenzando con las estrellas. Luego conecten las estrellas para completar el dibujo.

COMPARTAN

La fuerza de gravedad de la Tierra nos mantiene a nosotros y a nuestras cosas aquí en el suelo. Estimule a su niño/a a contar o a escribir un cuento extravagante sobre el día en que la fuerza de gravedad desaparezca lentamente. Estimule descripciones vívidas de los eventos que ocurren.

INTRODUCING THE PAIR-IT BOOKS

Display both books and have students read the titles. Explain that a challenge is something that is hard to do, such as compete in the Olympics. Write *challenge* in a word web on the board and ask students to suggest words or phrases for the web. You may want to prompt them by asking what things are hard for people to do.

Simon's Big Challenge

Simon is very unhappy when his family moves from Chicago to a ranch in western South Dakota. He misses his friends and the sights and sounds of the big city. But through an act of courage and caring, Simon discovers he can make friends anywhere.

Key Vocabulary

bridle	plummeted	scythe
filly	ranch	stable
gallop	saddle	stirrups
planetarium		

Objectives

Reading Strategy—Literary: Understanding character

Language Skill: Understanding past tense

Phonics/Word Study: Identifying diphthongs *ow, oy, oi*

For more phonics practice, see *Steck-Vaughn Phonics* Level C, Unit 4, pages 115–116.

Overcoming Challenges: The Life of Charles F. Bolden, Jr.

This nonfiction work details the life of Charles F. Bolden, Jr., who overcame prejudice and hardships to become an astronaut on the space shuttle *Columbia* in 1986.

Glossary Words

candidate	gravity	persevere
challenge	launch	persistence
determined	Mission Control	regulator
effort	obstacle	segregate
frustrating	overcome	uplifting
gauge		

Other Key Vocabulary

genius	satellite
orbit	shuttle

Objectives

Reading Strategy—Genre: Recognizing a biography

Language Skill: Identifying direct quotations

Phonics/Word Study: Understanding multiple-meaning words

For more word study practice, see *Steck-Vaughn Phonics* Level C, Unit 7, pages 191–192.

Additional Components

Audio Cassette: *Simon's Big Challenge/ Overcoming Challenges: The Life of Charles F. Bolden, Jr.*

Writing Masters, pages 105–108

Take Me Home Package

Other Resources About Challenges

First Biographies series, Steck-Vaughn

Brave as a Mountain Lion, Ann Herbert Scott

BEFORE READING

Display the book and have volunteers read the title and the table of contents aloud. Ask students if they can guess what Simon's big challenge is. Have them explain their predictions and write them on the board.

READING

To set a purpose for reading, ask students to find out what Jake discovers about Simon. Use questions such as these to guide the reading:

- *What are some of Simon's favorite activities in Chicago? (chapters 1–2)*
- *How is living on the ranch different from living in Chicago? (chapters 1–5)*
- *What are some of the animals that Simon sees in South Dakota? (chapters 3–5)*
- *What causes Simon to change his mind about living in South Dakota? (chapters 4–5)*

AFTER READING

Have volunteers review their predictions made in Before Reading. Ask if their predictions were disproved or confirmed. Discuss how the cover, title, and table of contents helped them to predict a story's outcome. Then encourage them to tell what Jake discovers about Simon.

Writing Activities

Simon's Plea
Materials: none

Have students write a letter from Simon to his parents persuading them not to move the family to South Dakota. As an option you may have students write a letter from Jerry to Simon persuading him to be open-minded about moving to South Dakota.

Dear Diary
Materials: none

Have one partner pretend to be Simon and the other, Jerry. Students can then write a diary entry for their character for two days: the day the family leaves for South Dakota and the day the boys meet Jake and the horses. Encourage students to tell the events of the day and how the character feels about the events. Then have partners discuss how their diary entries are alike and different.

MINI LESSONS

■ READING STRATEGY
Literary: Understanding Character

Explain that the people (and sometimes animals) in a story are called characters. Ask students to name the characters in *Simon's Big Challenge* and to describe the characters in a few words. Then tell students that just as real people change, the characters in a story may change. Have students identify how Simon and Jake change and tell what causes the changes.

■ LANGUAGE SKILL
Understanding Past Tense

Write *rush, look,* and *frown* on the board and ask how the words are alike. Lead students to see that these verbs tell about something happening now, or in the present. Ask students how they can change the verbs to show that the action happened in the past *(add -ed)*. Point out that some words do not follow this rule. Discuss *reply/replied, say/said,* and *fall/fell.* Ask students to find examples of verbs in the story that tell about action in the past.

PHONICS/WORD STUDY

Identifying Diphthongs *ow, oy, oi*
Write *town, boy,* and *oil* on the board, each in the center of a separate word web. Have volunteers read aloud the words. Explain that the letters *ow* can stand for the sound in *town* and that the letters *oy* and *oi* can stand for the same vowel sound, which is in *boy* and *oil.* Have small groups of students copy the webs. Then invite groups to add words with these sounds and spellings to the webs. Challenge students to find the word in the book that has *ow* and *oy* *(cowboy).*

Overcoming Challenges

The Life of Charles F. Bolden, Jr.

BEFORE READING

Encourage students to examine the cover and pictures of the book. Ask students what challenges Charles Bolden, Jr., may have faced. Have students write *Charles's Challenges* at the top of a sheet of paper and list the challenges as they read.

READING

To set a purpose for reading, ask students to find out the different kinds of work that Charles Bolden has done. Use questions such as the following to guide the reading:

- *What was life aboard* Columbia *like? (chapters 2–3)*
- *How did other people help Charles overcome challenges? (chapters 1, 4–6)*
- *What did Charles do to overcome challenges? (chapters 2–5)*
- *As Charles faced the different challenges, what are some of the ways he felt? (chapters 1–6)*

AFTER READING

Have students share the list of challenges that they made as they read the book. Discuss the different challenges that Charles encountered and what he did to overcome them.

Writing Activities

Interviewing Charles
Materials: encyclopedias, Internet access (optional)

Have partners research the kinds of experiments astronauts do while they are in space. Some students may want to use the NASA website (http://www.nasa.gov) to find information about current space exploration. Have students write a one-page report about what they learned. Allow time for students to discuss their reports and present them orally.

"Charles as a Child" Poem
Materials: none

Have students write Charles in the center of a word web, and sees, hears, thinks, and dreams as branches. Have them brainstorm ideas about what Charles may have seen, heard, thought, and dreamed about when he was a child. Invite them to use their ideas to write a poem about Charles.

> *He was Little Charles.*
> *He thought about* _____.
> *He saw* _____.
> *He heard* _____.
> *He dreamed about* _____.

MINI LESSONS

■ READING STRATEGY

Genre: Recognizing a Biography

Remind students that a biography is a story that tells the true story of someone's life. Ask students what clues tell them that this book is a biography. Then ask students to suggest elements that make up a good biography, such as major accomplishments, obstacles overcome, and a description of several events in the person's life. On chart paper write students' ideas for reference as they read and write other biographies.

■ LANGUAGE SKILL

Identifying Direct Quotations

Explain that a speaker's exact words are called a quotation and that quotations are surrounded with quotation marks. Have students turn to page 10 and invite a volunteer to read the first three sentences aloud. Ask students to identify the direct quotation. Then have students identify the quotations on pages 11 and 13 and explain why they are direct quotations.

PHONICS/WORD STUDY

Understanding Multiple-Meaning Words

Write the word *fly* on the board and elicit two meanings for the word. Explain to students that many words have more than one meaning. Then have partners work together to locate the following story words in a dictionary, read the meanings, and make up sentences using both meaning: *space, shuttle, roll, launch,* and *floats.*

Tying the Pair Together

Display *Simon's Big Challenge* and *Overcoming Challenges: The Life of Charles F. Bolden, Jr.*, and ask students to tell which book is fiction and which is nonfiction. Invite volunteers to tell how the main characters in the two books are alike and different. Write their responses in a Venn diagram on the board.

Geography: Investigating Places
Materials: physical map of North America, encyclopedias, almanac

Have students locate on a map Martin, South Dakota, and Columbia, South Carolina. Then have students find natural features near each location, such as the Badlands National Park near Martin, and Lake Marion near Columbia. Have partners use research materials to find out what there is to see and do in or near these places. Have partners present an oral report about the places.

Social Studies: Challenges Scrapbook
Materials: variety of newspapers and news magazines (past or current), glue, scissors

Provide small groups of students with a collection of news magazines and newspapers. Invite students to look through the materials and cut out stories about people who have overcome obstacles. Have students make a scrapbook of articles and pictures. Encourage students to list each person's challenges next to the article.

Drama: Wax Museum Play
Materials: encyclopedias and other history resources, prop materials (optional)

Invite students to portray figures in a wax museum. Have students research people who have overcome challenges—for example, Helen Keller, César Chavez, and Jackie Robinson. Have one student act as the museum guide and the other students as wax statues of their character. The guide introduces each statue, which "comes alive" and tells the audience about overcoming challenges. If possible, allow students to make simple props and then present their play.

Creative Arts: My Goals Poster
Materials: 12"× 12" posterboard squares, markers, colored pencils

Discuss goals that students might have for themselves and the challenges they might have to face to accomplish those goals. Then invite each student to create a posterboard square to show something he or she would like to do or become. Display the squares around the room and encourage students to discuss their posters with classmates.

ASSESSMENT

- Ask students what challenges the main characters in both books face and how they overcome these obstacles.
- Briefly retell a story that students have previously read and have them identify and describe the characters.
- Ask how a biography is different from a story about a fictional character.
- Review samples of students' writings to assess comprehension of what they read.
- Use informal conferencing with students to assess comprehension and skill growth.

For further assessment see the checklist on pages 109–111.

Home Activities

Copy and distribute to students the *Take It Home* activity master on page 103 (English) or page 104 (Spanish). Invite students to ask family members to discuss people they have known who have overcome obstacles to meet goals.

Dear Family of _____ ,

ACTIVITIES ABOUT OVERCOMING CHALLENGES

Your child has been reading about overcoming challenges. In *Simon's Big Challenge*, a young boy and his family move from Chicago to a ranch in South Dakota. At first Simon is unhappy, but he soon rises to the challenges of his new lifestyle. The companion book, *Overcoming Challenges: The Life of Charles F. Bolden, Jr.*, describes how Bolden overcame hardships and prejudice to become an astronaut. To help your child learn more about overcoming challenges, use the activities below.

BOOKS ABOUT OVERCOMING CHALLENGES

Help your child learn more about overcoming challenges by visiting the library. Check out and discuss books such as *Challenge at Second Base* by Matt Christopher and *Chicken Soup for the Kid's Soul: 101 Stories of Courage, Hope, and Laughter* by Jack Canfield. The latter is full of thought-provoking stories to discuss with your child.

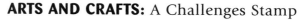

ARTS AND CRAFTS: A Challenges Stamp

Materials: 6″ × 6″ square of unlined paper, markers or colored pencils

Postage stamps often honor people who have overcome challenges. Invite your child to design a postage stamp honoring someone who has overcome challenges. Ask your child to draw the stamp on one side of a square piece of paper, write information about the person on the back, and share the stamp with other family members.

MOVIES AND MORE

Watch movies such as *Treasure Island* and *Apollo 13* with your child. Talk about the challenges that the characters have to overcome and how the characters show courage.

SHARE

Help your child think about times when he or she has overcome a challenge. For example, your child may have learned to do something he or she found difficult. Talk with your child about how it felt to overcome the challenge.

Estimada familia de _____,

ACTIVIDADES ACERCA DE CÓMO SUPERAR DESAFÍOS

Su niño/a ha estado leyendo sobre cómo superar desafíos. En *Simon's Big Challenge,* un niño pequeño y su familia se mudan de Chicago a un rancho en Dakota del Sur. Al comienzo, Simon se siente desdichado, pero pronto vence los desafíos de su nueva vida. El libro compañero, *Overcoming Challenges: The Life of Charles F. Bolden, Jr.,* describe cómo superó sus penurias y prejuicios para transformarse en un astronauta. Para ayudarle a su niño/a a superar desafíos, utilice las actividades que siguen.

LIBROS ACERCA DE CÓMO SUPERAR DESAFÍOS

Ayude a su niño/a a aprender más sobre cómo superar desafíos visitando la biblioteca. Saquen prestado y conversen sobre libros tales como *Challenge at Second Base* por Matt Christopher y *Chicken Soup for the Kid's Soul: 101 Stories of Courage, Hope, and Laughter* por Jack Canfield. Este último está lleno de cuentos que estimulan el pensamiento para que converse con su niño/a.

ARTE Y ARTESANÍA: Un sello de desafíos

Materiales: un cuadrado de papel sin líneas de 6 pulgadas por 6 pulgadas, marcadores o lápices de colores

Los sellos de correos frecuentemente honran a la gente que ha superado dificultades. Invite a su niño/a a disenar un sello de correo honrando una persoña que ha superado desafios. Pídale a su niño/a que dibuje un sello a un lado de un cuadrado de papel, que escriba la información sobre la persona al reverso y que comparta el sello con otros miembros de la familia.

PELÍCULAS Y MÁS

Vea películas tales como *Treasure Island* y *Apollo 13* con su niño/a. Conversen sobre los desafíos que tienen que superar los personajes y cómo estos muestran su valentía.

COMPARTAN

Ayúdele a su niño/a a pensar en situaciones en que ha tenido que superar un desafío. Por ejemplo, su niño/a puede haber aprendido a hacer algo que le ha sido difícil. Conversen acerca de lo que sintió cuando superó la dificultad.

Name _____

Use the diagram to compare and contrast a pair of books. Fill in the blanks to tell how the books are different and how they are alike.

Title _____

Different

Alike

Title _____

Different

Name _____

Choose a nonfiction book that you read. In each oval, write new information you learned about the topic. You can use the information to plan a report.

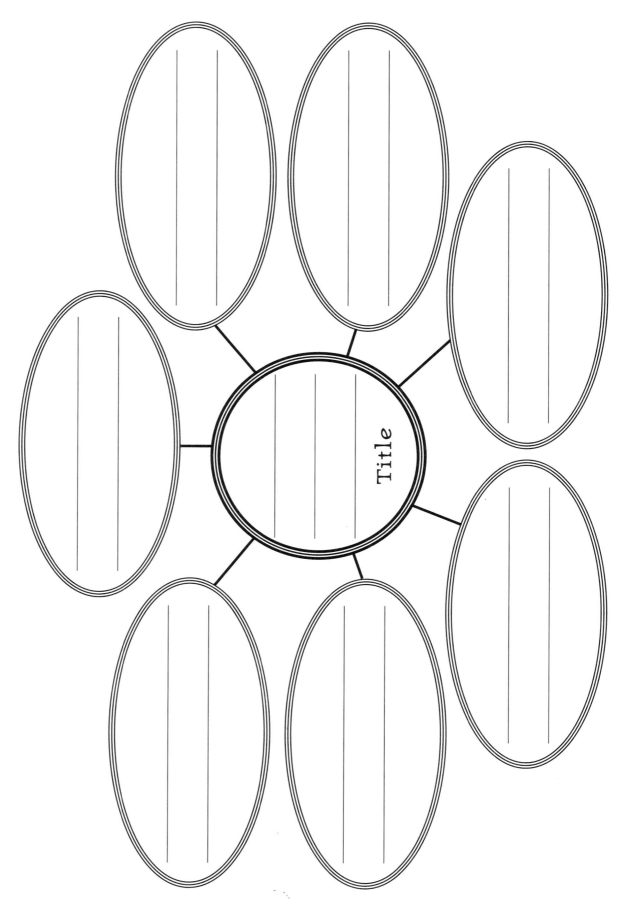

Title

Using New Information

Name

Use the outline to retell the events of a fiction book you read.

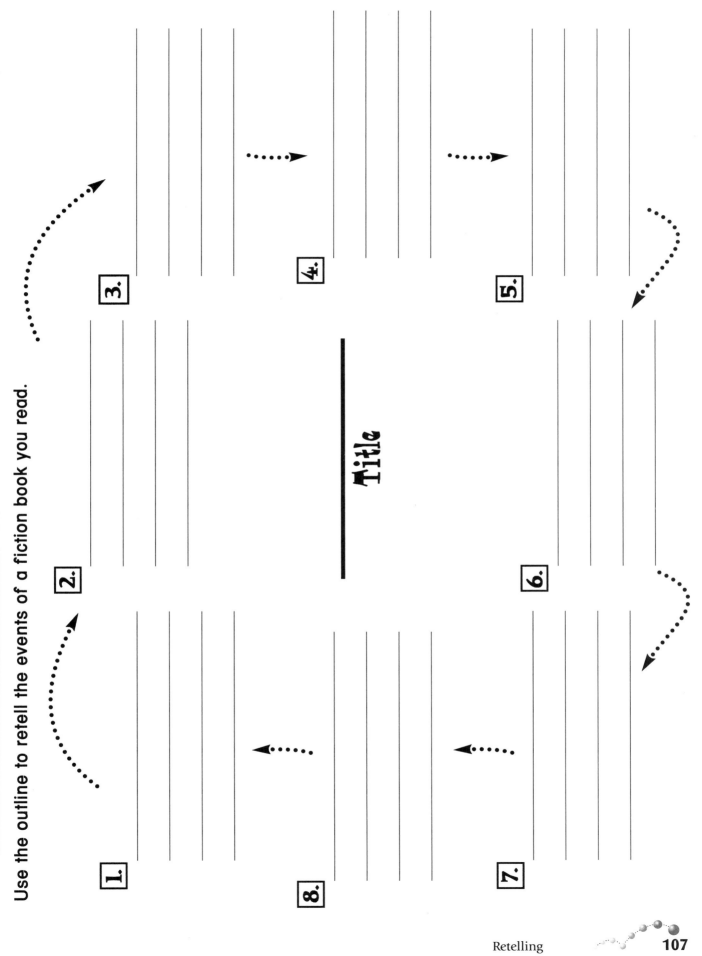

Title

1.

2.

3.

4.

5.

6.

7.

8.

Name _____

Choose a book that you read. First list the clues you already knew, then list the new clues that you read in the book. Add the clues together to draw your own conclusions.

Title _____

Clues I Already Knew

Book Clues

Conclusions

+

=

Drawing Conclusions

STECK-VAUGHN PAIR-IT BOOKS®
Checklist for Informal Assessment (Part I)

Student's Name _____

Reading Appreciation	Comments	Date
Shares books with others		
Selects books for personal needs and interests		
Chooses to read independently		
Participates actively in shared reading activities		
Integrates personal experiences into reading		

Reading Strategies	Comments	Date
Reads with phrasing, stress, and fluency		
Rereads to search and self-correct		
Uses context clues to determine meaning		
Uses text, illustrations, and photographs to make predictions		
Uses photographs to gain information		
Classifies and categorizes information		
Distinguishes between fantasy and fact		
Identifies cause/effect relationships		
Recognizes problem/solution relationships		
Identifies sequence of events		
Follows steps in a process		
Identifies main ideas and details		
Makes inferences		
Draws conclusions		
Applies information		
Summarizes text		

Literary Concepts	Comments	Date
Understands dialogue		
Identifies author's purpose		
Distinguishes narration from exposition		
Understands setting		
Understands character		

Genre Recognition	Comments	Date
Recognizes fiction		
Recognizes nonfiction		
Recognizes a journal entry		
Recognizes a diary entry		
Recognizes a biography		
Recognizes a fantasy		
Recognizes a mystery		
Recognizes a pourquoi tale		
Recognizes historical fiction		
Recognizes humorous fiction		

STECK-VAUGHN PAIR-IT BOOKS®
Checklist for Informal Assessment (Part II)

Student's Name _____

Study Skills	Comments	Date
Reads and follows directions		
Uses parts of a book: table of contents, glossary, index		
Scans for information		
Uses text features and structure		
Interprets photograph captions		
Interprets diagrams		
Uses maps		
Interprets tables		
Interprets timelines		

Language Skills	Comments	Date
Recognizes onomatopoeia		
Identifies possessive form of nouns		
Understands specialized language		
Distinguishes common and proper nouns		
Recognizes irregular verb forms		
Distinguishes past and present tense		
Recognizes action and linking verbs		
Forms irregular plurals		
Uses figurative language		
Uses helping verbs *has* and *have* correctly		
Understands contractions		
Uses synonyms/antonyms		
Recognizes present tense		
Recognizes past tense		
Identifies comparatives and superlatives		
Identifies and uses adjectives		
Distinguishes between points of view		
Understands pronouns and antecedents		
Identifies adverbs		
Identifies proper nouns and adjectives		
Understands dialogue		
Uses commas in a series correctly		
Understands acronyms		
Identifies compound predicates		
Identifies direct quotations		

STECK-VAUGHN PAIR-IT BOOKS®
Checklist for Informal Assessment (Part III)

Student's Name _____

Phonics/Word Study

	Comments	Date
Uses initial and final consonant sounds to decode unfamiliar words		
Uses vowel sounds to decode unfamiliar words		
Uses sounds of consonant blends and digraphs to decode unfamiliar words		
Uses sounds of vowel digraphs and diphthongs to decode unfamiliar words		
Recognizes three sounds of *s*		
Uses hard and soft *c* and *g* sounds		
Identifies *r*-controlled vowels		
Identifies silent consonants		
Identifies *y* used as a vowel		
Recognizes plurals		
Recognizes inflectional endings		
Understands homonyms		
Identifies multiple-meaning words		
Appreciates word origins		
Identifies compound words		
Recognizes suffixes and prefixes in words		
Identifies word roots		
Recognizes and identifies syllables		

Writing Skills

	Comments	Date
Generates and narrows topics for writing		
Uses information from text in writing		
Uses main idea/details in writing		
Uses a wide range of vocabulary in writing		
Uses capitalization correctly		
Uses punctuation correctly		
Organizes ideas		
Uses a variety of sentence structures		
Proofreads writing		

INDEX